Praise for *Partnering with the CIO*

"The authors demonstrate a deep understanding of the challenges facing CIOs who are making tough investment decisions every day and the opportunity for IT vendors who understand both sides of the equation. This book should be read by everyone involved in buying or selling IT resources."

—Ellen Kitzis
VP Research, Gartner; co-author
of *The New CIO Leader*

"*Partnering with the CIO* is filled with practical insights from a who's who list of CIOs. It's a must read for IT vendor management and their sales forces."

—Gary Beach
Publisher, *CIO* magazine

"Vendors still don't get the CIO animal. CIOs are buried with vague, impersonal, and untargeted pitches on a daily basis from providers who don't understand their business, their industry, and what really makes them tick. Read this book and you will separate yourself and your company from the pack."

—David C. Munn
President and CEO, Information
Technology Services Marketing
Association

"Finally, a book about IT sales written from the customer's viewpoint. This book makes the case for adopting customer-centric sales and marketing strategies in the enterprise software industry."

> —Don Peppers and Martha Rogers, PhD
> co-founders of the Peppers & Rogers Group;
> co-authors of *The One to One Future*,
> *Enterprise One to One*, and *Return on Customer*

PARTNERING
WITH THE CIO

THE FUTURE OF **IT SALES**
SEEN THROUGH THE EYES
OF **KEY DECISION MAKERS**

PARTNERING
WITH THE CIO

MICHAEL MINELLI
MIKE BARLOW

BICENTENNIAL
1807
WILEY
2007
BICENTENNIAL

John Wiley & Sons, Inc.

Published by John Wiley & Sons, Inc., Hoboken, New Jersey.
Published simultaneously in Canada.

Wiley Bicentennial Logo: Richard J. Pacifico

For general information on our other products and services or for technical support, please contact our Customer Care Department within the United States at (800) 762-2974, outside the United States at (317) 572-3993 or fax (317) 572-4002.

Wiley also publishes its books in a variety of electronic formats. Some content that appears in print may not be available in electronic books. For more information about Wiley products, visit our web site at www.wiley.com.

Library of Congress Cataloging-in-Publication Data:

Minelli, Michael, 1974–
    Partnering with the CIO : the future of IT sales seen through the eyes of key decision makers / Michael Minelli, Mike Barlow.
        p.   cm.
    Includes bibliographical references and index.
    ISBN 978-0-470-12244-0 (cloth)
        1. Chief information officers.   2. Information technology—Economic aspects.
    3. Information technology—Management.   I. Barlow, Mike.   II. Title.
    HD30.2.M56   2007
    004.068'8—dc22   2007004978

Printed in the United States of America.

10   9   8   7   6   5   4   3   2   1

For Jenny, Jack, and Madeline
and
For Darlene, Janine, and Paul

CONTENTS

FOREWORD

As the CIO Role Changes and Evolves, IT Suppliers Must Update Their Strategies

The CIO role has undergone a dramatic transformation since its introduction to the mainstream business world more than 20 years ago.

Today, in the most advanced businesses, the CIO (chief information officer) is a true *officer* of the company, co-accountable with the rest of the management team for the competitive growth and strategic success of the business, fully capable of proactively envisioning business opportunities and collaboratively acting upon them.

Even in less forward-looking companies, CIOs are critical strategic contributors to business success, helping to understand and drive new business processes that enable their businesses to reach their bottom line goals.

Modern CIOs carry enormous burdens and responsibilities. They confront staff shortages, excruciating budgetary pressures, and escalating demands from virtually every functional area of their organizations. They see themselves locked in seemingly endless cycles of reinforcing the business value of IT and defending the return on IT investments.

In this type of environment, it's easy to understand why the CIO has limited patience for IT vendors whose main focus is selling the latest, greatest product.

On the other hand, today's environment offers a vast range of fresh opportunities for IT suppliers who take the time to understand the CIO's challenges and who are willing to partner and build relationships with the CIO as an individual.

For IT suppliers, *selling* to the CIO is not an effective strategy. Selling tends to be a hit-and-run affair, a zero-sum game with winners and losers. That kind of selling may have worked in the past, but it certainly won't work today. CIOs have moved to the next level and they are looking for next-level relationships with their suppliers.

Smart IT suppliers learn how to *partner* with CIOs. They learn how to create a continuing stream of win-win scenarios in which the business objectives of all parties are achieved successfully over a period of many years.

As the CIO of CXO Media, producer of *CIO* and *CSO* magazines and the CIO Executive Council, I get my own daily share of mass-marketed e-mails, direct mails, and all too often, scattered, rambling voicemails from vendors who can only pretend to know something about me or my business. While the CIO role has evolved dramatically, the manner in which vendors approach the CIO has remained primitive and uninspired.

In my role as founding general manager of the CIO Executive Council, a professional, member-driven organization focused on advancing the CIO profession, I have the tremendous pleasure and honor of speaking daily with CIOs about their strategic goals and objectives. Time and time again, relationships with vendors top their list of challenges and concerns.

The most common phrase I hear—not an encouraging phrase, to be sure—is that most vendors are "a necessary evil." This hardly sounds like the beginning of a beautiful relationship.

CIOs all over the world tell me that the old rules of selling don't work anymore and that the traditional sales paradigm has to change. Our own internal research tells us that CIOs' confidence in the vendor community's ability to deliver is on a sharp decline. A CIO Executive Council survey taken in April 2006 shows that 8 out of 10 CIOs believe that vendors overstate their service capabilities. Similarly, a poll taken in September 2006 shows more than half of CIOs have low confidence in software vendors.

Clearly, vendors need a new strategy. Instead of viewing CIOs as targets, they should first view them as highly capable executives with very difficult jobs. CIOs will be receptive to vendors who are willing to put time and effort into getting to know them and their businesses.

IT vendors need to apply more resources researching their customers and potential customers so they can assemble an accurate picture of the CIO's true business needs. Investments in research and other relationship-building activities almost always generate impressive rewards over time.

Members of the CIO Executive Council agree with virtual unanimity that the best way for an IT supplier to get in the door is through a referral from a trusted peer. The quickest way to close that door permanently is through a negative referral from a frustrated peer.

Our U.S. members alone control more than $90 billion in annual IT spending. The vendor community cannot afford to remain stuck in the past. There's just too much at stake.

As their roles and responsibilities become increasingly complex, modern CIOs need feedback and support from their peers. And they need better support and improved services from the vendor community.

That's the heart of the argument in *Partnering with the CIO*. IT suppliers must adopt new sales strategies to match the needs of their CIO customers, today and tomorrow.

Partnering with the CIO takes a unique approach in that it asks CIOs directly to describe their experiences as sales targets and gathers their suggestions for ways in which IT vendors can improve their sales processes. It is a must-read for anyone who wants to gain better insight into the CIO's mind.

—Mark Hall
Founding General Manager,
CIO Executive Council

The CIO Executive Council is a professional, member-driven organization largely focused on advancing the CIO profession. Founded by the creators and readers of CIO magazine in April 2004, the organization now boasts more than 400 members worldwide. For detailed information, please visit www.cioexecutivecouncil.com.

ACKNOWLEDGMENTS

Since this book is essentially a work of journalism and reportage, we could not have written it without tapping into the knowledge, experience, and wisdom of many expert sources. To them we are indebted deeply. We thank them sincerely for their time, their energy, their support, and their patience.

We are especially thankful for the aid and guidance provided to us by Mark Hall, founding general manager of the CIO Executive Council, and Karen Fogerty, director of external relations at CXO Media.

Over the course of researching and writing this book, we benefited greatly from the assistance of many wonderful friends and colleagues, including Beverly Brown, Kathy Council, Jim Davis, Peter Dillman, Suzanne Fiero, John Foley, Sean Gargan, Annette Green, Bonnie Kantor, Amy Kirby, Jack LoBianco, Michelle Mac, Britton Manasco, Mike Marselle, Pamela Meek, Faye Merrideth, Helju Nommik, Julie Platt, John Rinello, Martino Roselli, Dan Spillett, Margo Stutesman, and Robert Szczerba.

The substance of this book is derived mainly from interviews with CIOs and other technology executives at numerous organizations. We would not have been able to write *Partnering with the CIO* without the active participation and cooperation of Bill Babcock, Bruce Barnes, Mike Blake,

Marcia Bohannon, Paul Cosgrave, Myles Cyr, Brian Dearth, Jeri Dunn, Gary Fink, Mary Finlay, Michael Friedenberg, Michelle Garvey, Suzanne Gordon, Avi Halutz, Ray Hill, David King, Ellen Kitzis, Harvey Koeppel, Mark Lutchen, Brian Margolies, Steve McDowell, Brad Miller, David Munn, Jeffrey Neville, Mark Polansky, Ron Rose, Alec Palmer, David Read, Emry Sisson, Gregory Smith, William Sweeney, Bob Turner, John von Stein, Fred Wedley, Simon Wiggins, and Paul Zazzera.

We owe special thanks to Aaron Overington, who prepared the charts and graphics for this book.

All writers, of course, need many additional pairs of eyes. We were especially fortunate to work with Edith G. Barlow, whose careful copy editing and useful suggestions greatly improved the quality of our manuscript. We also thank Matthew Holt, Jessica Campilango, and Kate Lindsay, our editors at John Wiley & Sons, who had faith in the value of our project and were patient when we missed our deadlines. And special thanks to the staff of Cape Cod Compositors for their creativity and attention to detail.

Most of all, we thank our families, who put up with long nights of writing, endless phone calls, and lost weekends of heavy editing.

From Selling to Partnering

The seed kernel of this book is a brief anecdote told to us by Paul Zazzera, a former senior vice president and chief information officer at Time, Inc.

A tall, solidly built man with silver hair and a thick mustache, he is passionate about the need for IT to be perceived—and to behave—as a business.

Zazzera was traveling on a nonstop transcontinental flight when an IT sales rep sat down next to him and spent the next several hours bending his ear with a nonstop sales pitch.

How the rep had tracked down Zazzera's flight and had wangled himself into a neighboring seat remains a mystery. But the story got us wondering if other CIOs had similar experiences with IT reps whose zeal to pitch led them to such extremes.

It turned out that plenty of CIOs had even worse stories to share with us. So we decided to write a book. We planned to call our book *Buzz Off.* Essentially it would be a compilation of horror stories told by CIOs, a best of the worst collection for the amusement of IT insiders.

But when we told our CIO friends about the book, they immediately became very serious. Sternly and solemnly they said, "You know, this disconnect between the buyers and sellers of IT is a significant problem. You shouldn't joke about it."

Even the most jovial CIOs used terms such as "fundamentally broken" and "profoundly illogical" to describe the current state of relations between IT sales reps and their prospects.

So we shifted our focus. *Buzz Off* morphed into *Selling to the CIO*. The new title reflected our sincere desire to explain exactly what had gone wrong with the IT sales process and to suggest potential ways for repairing the damage.

After about a dozen interviews, however, we realized that our title needed another revision. Without exception, the CIOs we interviewed said they didn't want IT suppliers to "sell" them IT products and services.

Instead, the CIOs want IT suppliers to partner with them by understanding the specific business needs of their organizations and by providing technology engineered to address those specific needs. Furthermore, the CIOs we interviewed want IT sales reps to talk less about technology and talk more about business value.

The CIOs we interviewed also want IT sales reps to kick their habit of offering last-minute, end-of-quarter or end-of-year discounts as incentives to close deals for products without first proving how those products will create value for the buyer.

Most important, the CIOs want IT suppliers to stop treating them like prom dates and start treating them as long-term partners in a continually evolving business relationship.

After analyzing the transcripts from our initial interviews, we realized that our job as authors was discovering and writing about the many ways in which IT suppliers can part-ner meaningfully with CIOs. And that's how the book's title became *Partnering with the CIO*.

The CIO's Inner Circle

CIOs spoke tantalizingly about an "inner circle" of trusted suppliers they turn to when facing critical issues. To be fair, not every CIO used the exact term "inner circle." Some used phrases such as "a select group of vendors I especially trust" or "a handful of salespeople who really know me and truly understand the situations I'm in."

Despite variations in phraseology, almost every CIO we interviewed acknowledged the existence of a small group of IT suppliers and consultants who had gradually earned the CIO's trust.

Since no two CIOs had the same inner circle, there's no point in naming names. Instead, let's take a good look at the characteristics required for membership in this elite club.

Unlike the Order of Skull and Bones, the notoriously secret society based at Yale University, membership in the CIO's inner circle isn't limited to bluebloods or captains of the rowing team. That's the good news.

The bad news is that CIOs are extremely picky and often impatient. They find meaningless chatter and obvious sales tactics irritating. They can easily spot the difference between someone who merely wants to sell and someone who sincerely wants to help them.

You don't have to be telepathic to get inside the CIO's head. When a CIO sizes up a salesperson, there are only two questions on his mind: "Can you help me?" and "Can I trust you?"

"You're Gonna Need a Bigger Boat"

Information technology has become the indispensable tool of our age. It would be *extremely difficult* to imagine our society functioning at its current level of modernity without the capabilities routinely provided by IT. It would be *impossible* to imagine our interconnected global economy functioning without IT.

Information technology already surrounds us. It has achieved ubiquity. Like indoor plumbing and central heating, IT is now universally accepted and expected. It's not going away.

Over the next three decades, IT will become so thoroughly woven into our lives that the boundaries between biology and IT will become essentially meaningless.

Barring some worldwide cataclysm, the demand for IT will continue rising for the rest of the twenty-first century.

So why aren't IT suppliers jumping for joy? Because their lives are harder than ever! Despite rising demand, it's more difficult to sell IT products and services than ever before. Here are two primary reasons for the sense of discomfort felt by IT suppliers:

1. Unyielding downward pressure on pricing.

2. Steadily increasing expectations.

Put those two reasons together and you get an environment that makes selling downright difficult. Even as demand skyrockets, IT has become a buyer's market.

There's a third reason for the pain experienced by IT suppliers. This third reason is far more complex than the first two, and that's why we devote the rest of this book to examining it. Here it is:

3. A fundamental disconnect has occurred between the IT supplier community and the IT consumer community.

We're not exactly sure when the gap became visible, but it's been widening steadily for about the past 15 years. Far from crossing the chasm, many IT suppliers have actually been digging themselves into a deeper hole.

Our educated guess is that the fissure between the two communities won't begin narrowing until everything related to IT is bought and sold as a service. In the meantime, this book helps you navigate the rough waters ahead.

We've all seen the movie *Jaws* seven or eight times, right? Remember when Chief Brody steps back into the cabin after seeing the shark? He says, "You're gonna need a bigger boat."

That could have been the subtitle of this book. Like Chief Brody, we've seen the problem with our own eyes—and we know it's huge.

Surrender Is Not an Option

If you sell IT products or IT-related services, this book is for you. It contains prudent tactical advice culled from hours of interviews with CIOs and senior technology executives representing dozens of corporations. We solemnly promise that each chapter includes news you can use.

This book also contains high-level strategic counsel based on a synthesis of our interviews and our own years of experience in the business. Of the many messages that emerged from our research, here are three that you need to know immediately.

1. The CIO faces real business problems. Find out what those real problems are, help the CIO prioritize them, help the CIO solve them, and stick around during the delivery phase.

2. Help the CIO create competitive advantages for his or her organization.

3. CIOs are looking for strategic relationships. They are desperately seeking long-term business partners. If you don't engage the CIO in a long-term, strategic business relationship, someone else will.

Let's put it even more bluntly: IT suppliers who fail to understand the CIO's new perspective on value and who do not update their sales processes to keep pace with the CIO's changing environment will surrender the most profitable parts of their business.

You have a choice, but it's a stark one. You can be a strategic partner, or you can be a commodity.

Experience versus Expertise

David L. King is senior vice president and CIO at Regal Entertainment Group, the nation's largest chain of movie theaters. Today the motion picture industry is going through its largest transition since talkies replaced silent movies in the late 1920s. This time around, digital media is replacing film. As a result, IT is moving from a supporting role in the back office to a leading role on the big screen.

Based in Knoxville, Tennessee, Regal is at the forefront of the digital movie revolution. As the owner-operator of 560 multiplex theaters, Regal's technology challenges are enormous. On average, each multiplex has 11 screens showing five feature-length movies daily, 365 days a year. In digital format, each feature is about 300 to 400 gigabytes (GBs). The coming attractions add another 40 GBs to the load of information that must be distributed across Regal's chain of cinemas.

"A lot of the technology required to accomplish all this on a routine basis doesn't exist yet," says King.

In this type of transformational environment, King looks for IT suppliers who are ready, willing, and able to serve as strategic partners. The challenge for King is identifying which suppliers are truly committed to long-term relationships and which suppliers are just seeking short-term wins.

There are two basic requirements for being considered as a strategic partner: enough experience to handle a complex, transformational engagement and enough depth to commit the spectrum of resources necessary to follow through successfully on a multiyear project.

In some selling scenarios, it's easy to spot which suppliers can talk the talk, but can't walk the walk. "Usually you pick up on it immediately," says King. "All you have to do is describe some specific problems and ask the vendors how they solve those problems."

Since any reasonably energetic sales rep with a Web browser and an Internet connection can acquire enough information to chat about practically any technical subject, it's important for King to determine quickly if the rep's domain expertise is built on a solid foundation of real experience or conjured up from an all-nighter of caffeine and Google.

Expertise is not the same as experience. Expertise can be picked up on the ride from the airport to the customer's office. Experience develops over time—and it's hard to fake.

Smart sales reps try to stay out of situations in which their expertise doesn't match their experience. And CIOs like King try to avoid dealing with vendors who make a habit of sending people lacking real-world experience into meetings.

What happens when King is looking for a strategic partner and the vendor sends over a team without the right level of experience?

"I'll be courteous, but I'll bring the meeting to a close fairly quickly," says King. "Then I'll meet with my people and find out why they failed to qualify that vendor appropriately. If I feel that the sales rep tried to mislead us, I'll probably call one of the vendor's senior execs and describe what happened."

If it turns out that that sales rep is just naturally aggressive, King says he usually gives the vendor a second chance to make the pitch with another rep.

If King determines that the vendor's corporate culture encourages the sales force to engage in inappropriately aggressive or misleading behavior, he's not shy about sharing his observations with friends and colleagues throughout the CIO community. "I'll let everyone in my network know what happened," says King.

For CIOs, sharing stories about misbehaving vendors isn't about getting revenge—it's a matter of survival. "You rely on vendors and partners to help you accomplish your mission," says King. "Every time you select a vendor or a partner, your job is on the line."

It's critical for vendors to understand the extent to which CIOs depend on them. It's also critical for vendors to remember that when CIOs change jobs, they bring their memories with them.

CIOs base their impressions of a vendor on their dealings with the vendor's sales force. If the sales force is consistently sending the wrong messages, the vendor's reputation will invariably suffer.

Levels of Commitment

A sales rep's ability to say "Been there, done that" weighs more heavily as a factor in the vendor selection process when the solution under consideration is critical to the business, says King.

"If the solution isn't critical, we might be willing to try something new with the vendor. But even then, the vendor will need to demonstrate some past success in doing new things with other customers or within other parts of our business," says King. "I'm really looking for signs of commitment. I want to know that the vendor will stick with us, and not get bored and disappear."

Not every relationship has to be strategic. King doesn't expect the same level of commitment from a vendor selling PC peripherals as he does from a vendor selling an enterprise financial management solution.

"We look for higher levels of commitment from vendors supplying business-critical solutions. As the business process becomes more critical, our need to feel comfortable with the vendor increases," says King. "If we're talking about a commodity such as a computer mouse, then we don't need the same level of comfort with the vendor."

When King is interested in working with a vendor, he doesn't hesitate to explain precisely what he's seeking.

"Early in the sales cycle I try to describe the role that the vendor will be playing within our company. I'll describe the vendor's responsibilities, the level of service we're expecting, and the kinds of results we're looking to achieve," says King. "And I'll ask the vendor, 'Can you fill this role? Where have you done this before?'"

Chapter ONE

The Once and Future CIO

"In the past, hundreds of billions of IT dollars were wasted either because no metrics were used, or worse, because the wrong metrics were used."

Mark Lutchen

Former Global CIO of PricewaterhouseCoopers and currently Senior Practice Partner for PwC's IT Effectiveness Initiative; author of *Managing IT as a Business*

Yesterday, Today, and Beyond

Before we can talk about partnering with the CIO, we first need to understand how the role of the CIO developed. Second, we need to get a clear fix on where the CIO stands today. Third, we need to plot a likely trajectory for the next generation of CIOs—because they are the IT customers of the future!

Those of us who came of age during the era of FORTRAN and COBOL know in our bones how much the IT universe has changed over the past 35 years. If you're old enough to remember writing programs on punch cards, you will also remember that in the 1970s and 1980s, most organizations didn't spend a lot of time or energy thinking about IT.

They weren't even calling it IT back then; they called it IS, the acronym for information services. At most companies, IS budgets represented mere fractions of annual spending—certainly not enough to warrant close attention from senior executives or directors.

The IS manager was a creature of this semiopaque, laissez faire environment. He (or, rarely, she) was not considered a player in any corporate sense. The IS manager was a technical person whose primary job was making sure the company's mainframe computers got fixed when they broke down. Gradually, as terminals began appearing on desks, the IS manager's job expanded to include making sure the terminals got fixed when they broke down.

The adoption of client–server systems in the 1980s made life more interesting for the IS manager but didn't do much to raise his or her status in the corporate table of organization.

It wasn't until the mid-1990s, when organizations truly started to understand the strategic value of information, that IS began getting the respect it had long deserved. Suddenly everyone was talking about the Age of Information. Companies referred to themselves as "knowledge-driven." The global economy was an "information economy." We were "wired" citizens of a brave new "digital society."

If the "information superhighway" seemed like pure hype, other concepts such as the "killer app" and the "networked economy" struck a chord and helped define an era of radical change.

From the corporate perspective, the digital revolution transformed information from an inevitable by-product of routine transactions into a coveted asset with unlimited potential value.

The new focus on information elevated the role of the IS manager. Many companies began referring to their IS functions as IT, which suggested a broader scope and reflected the decade's infatuation with technology.

Soon it became apparent that IT was too important to be run by a mere manager. So the manager of IT became the director of IT. From there, it was a hop, skip, and jump to CIO (chief information officer).

Even when a company's CIO wasn't a full-fledged C-level executive, the prestigious title certainly indicated a higher rank than that of his or her predecessors.

When the title CIO was coined, the C-suite was still a lonely place. Sure, there was the CEO, the CFO, and maybe a COO. But you didn't have today's crowd of chiefs on the organization chart.

The first generation of CIOs wasn't jostling for elbow room with CMOs (chief marketing officers), CPOs (chief procurement officers), CCOs (chief customer officers), or CLOs (chief learning officers).

An Evolving Model

The earliest CIOs (let's call them CIO 1.0) were pioneers in the sense that there was no road map or precedent for them to follow. Whether they worked at Fortune 500 companies or Internet start-ups, they were creatures of the dot-com boom.

CIO 1.0 was the living embodiment of a new business model, based on the belief that information, if properly managed, would drive growth. In this model, IT was an essential component of business strategy.

The subsequent dot-com bust proved beyond doubt that the model needed work. Fortunately, its central principle survived the bust. That principle was simply this: Competitive organizations need world-class IT.

There was still plenty of debate about the intrinsic value of information, but nobody was disputing the basic argument that IT had ascended to the level of a core competency or that companies could not grow without an IT strategy firmly in place.

Despite the bust, the IT genie didn't go back into the bottle. Under intense pressure from a host of internal and external forces, CIO 1.0 evolved into CIO 2.0, not quite yet an emperor, but a significant player in the new economy.

The CIO of today is a leader. He or she plays a key role in the planning, development, and execution of company-wide strategy. CIO 2.0 is a "go to" person for achieving the company's primary strategic business goals—growth and profitability.

CIO 2.0 enjoys higher status than CIO 1.0 but shoulders far heavier responsibilities. If you're a CIO, you know exactly what we're talking about.

A Multiplicity of CIOs

CIO 3.0 might not be a single individual. Ellen Kitzis, Gartner, vice president of research, and co-author of *The New CIO Leader*, says that tomorrow's IT department won't be a monolithic organization.

"At Gartner we have a team that studies the future of IT organizations," says Dr. Kitzis. "In one of our scenarios, there are as many as three different organizations for IT. One organization focuses on utility and another focuses on business change projects. Another organization concentrates on innovation and strategy."

Would an enterprise with multiple IT organizations need multiple CIOs? Some of the IT organizations might be led by CIOs. But others might be led by executives of business units or functional areas that depend on IT resources. There might be an IT organization focused on utility, another focused on innovation, and yet another focused on business change projects.

Dr. Kitzis suggests that different IT organizations within the enterprise might have significantly different kinds of relationships with suppliers. For example, the IT organization responsible for utility probably would have relationships with fewer suppliers than the IT organization responsible for innovation and R&D (research and development).

"That's because the utility organization will be focused on building stable business processes, while the R&D

organization will be out there looking for edgy stuff and testing relationships with many suppliers," Dr. Kitzis explains.

The IT organization responsible for business change will be likely to form relationships with suppliers who understand a variety of business processes and business models.

If any of these scenarios plays out, the role of the IT sales rep might change dramatically. A single rep, or a single team of reps, simply wouldn't have the bandwidth required to successfully manage relationships across an enterprise with multiple IT departments, multiple CIOs, and decentralized decision-making processes.

On the other hand, the emergence of highly specialized IT organizations might make the sales rep's job much easier since each organization would have its own clearly defined goals and processes. It would be easier for the sales rep to identify the real needs and business challenges of each IT organization within the enterprise.

Ideally, IT sales reps would leverage their knowledge to create highly customized, perfectly tailored pitches for each organization. This would end the time-honored and generally despised practice of recycling generic sales presentations by adding two or three new slides and hoping the CIO doesn't notice.

A Strategic Mind-Set

Today's CIOs aren't paid to make tactical decisions. Instead, CIOs are paid to make decisions that will benefit their companies over the long term. Recognizing this, some companies are giving their CIOs new titles, such as senior vice president of business transformation or vice president of strategic development.

Make no mistake: Modern CIOs are strategists, and that means they need to be treated differently from how they were treated in the past when they were tacticians.

In his historical plays about King Henry IV, Shakespeare describes a situation that's relevant to our point. The king's son, Prince Hal, is a nasty juvenile delinquent. Hal's drinking buddy is Falstaff, an overweight knight who prefers carousing over fighting. Hal and Falstaff are best friends and partners in crime—until Hal's dad dies and Hal becomes king. As King Henry V, Hal is responsible for the safety of England. He becomes a different man—and cuts off his friendship with Falstaff. It's a sad moment on the stage, but it speaks to an inescapable truth. When someone's responsibilities are elevated, they change.

How much do they change? When someone moves from a management role into a leadership role, the change can be enormous. In "CIO to CEO," a white paper published by Korn/Ferry International, authors Mark Polansky and Simon Wiggins draw fascinating conclusions from an in-depth study based on data gathered from more than a half-million top executives (nearly 1,500 of whom were senior level IT execs). The data was mined and analyzed to develop "success profiles" for CEOs, COOs, and CIOs.

The study shows that successful CIOs tend to behave much like successful CEOs and COOs. There are some striking behavioral differences, of course, but the net takeaway is that many CIOs have adopted, or are in the process of adopting, styles of leadership and thinking that are very similar to those of the topmost executives.

How do the topmost executives generally behave?

- They focus on long-term objectives.

- They think in terms of profit and loss, rather than costs.

- They have a higher tolerance for ambiguity than lower-level executives, but will respond quickly and decisively when a situation demands swift action.

Our experience leads us to believe that these behavioral styles are gradually becoming the norm for CIOs. If you accept the premise of the Korn/Ferry white paper, CIOs who aspire to become COOs or CEOs have already embraced those behavioral styles. That's why a sales pitch that worked just fine yesterday isn't going to work tomorrow. The mindset of the target audience will have changed.

So here's our advice: When you're pitching to the CIO, act as though you're pitching to the CEO. More specifically, when you're talking to the CIO, remember that what you're really doing is preparing him or her for a meeting with the steering committee or board who is responsible for approving large-scale IT projects.

So if 80 percent of your pitch to the CIO is about the deal or about your company or about your platform—you're toast, dude!

The CIO is struggling to see the big picture and needs your help. So flip that old pitch on its head. Make sure that 80 percent of your conversation is about the business value you're going to create for the CIO's organization. Now you're talking the right language.

Yes, You *Are* Important

So far, we've highlighted changes in the CIO's role. We've looked at a variety of external and internal forces that are relentlessly transforming the CIO from a tech manager into a business executive.

But there's another critical force acting upon the CIO. That force is you, the IT supplier. You play a major role in shaping the CIO's perspective and determining his or her long-term success. At the end of the day, the CIO's performance is judged largely by how well your products perform and how well your organization supports the CIO's strategy.

Sometimes You Have to Ask

It's helpful to imagine the CIO as the conductor and the IT suppliers as members of the orchestra. If you play well, the CIO will get a standing ovation. The audience might not be aware of your contribution, but the conductor knows who is playing well—and who isn't.

As a supplier, you need to know the business priorities of every CIO you work with. If a CIO doesn't volunteer to share his or her priorities with you, then it's your job to ask for them. If you determine that a CIO isn't exactly sure about his or her business priorities, then help the CIO figure out what's really important—and what's not.

More often than not, you will find that the CIOs you deal with are eager to hear your opinions and happy to let you serve as their mentor. They want to trust you, and they want to have faith in your advice. Don't disappoint them, and never ever give them a reason not to trust you.

Your success depends on your ability to build and nurture long-term relationships with CIOs. Their success depends on their ability to develop long-term relationships with suppliers they trust.

It's not easy to build and maintain trusting relationships in a turbulent, ever-changing industry such as IT. But those relationships will be absolutely critical to sellers and buyers.

Share the CIO's Priorities

We're great fans of Mark Lutchen, the former Global CIO of PricewaterhouseCoopers (PwC). Lutchen is currently the senior practice partner for PwC's IT Effectiveness Initiative, which develops practical strategies for managing IT risks and optimizing IT investments. He is also the author of *Managing IT as a Business*, a no-nonsense guide for senior executives grappling with the challenges and opportunities created by technology.

In his book, Lutchen observes that the current trend in IT management is less of a great leap forward and more of "an inescapable return to reality. In the past, hundreds of billions of IT dollars were wasted either because no metrics were used, or worse, because the wrong metrics were used."

Lutchen outlines six critical steps for CIOs who are seeking a path through the wilderness of IT management. His six steps are also extremely useful for IT suppliers who want to share the vision and priorities of their CIO customers.

In fact, a wise supplier will embrace these six steps and actively assist the CIO as he or she follows the steps to their logical conclusion: an IT organization that is perfectly aligned with the goals and profitability drivers of its parent organization.

Here are Lutchen's six steps:

1. Bring IT into the mainstream of the enterprise.

2. Consider the IT organization as a stand-alone business unit (though not necessarily a profit center) that ad-

vances the agenda of both the corporate center and the various business units.

3. Link IT strategy to corporate strategy, but with a focus on practical execution rather than theory and idealized processes.

4. Require business units to define their IT needs and require IT to provide services through a methodology of rigorous relationship management.

5. Institutionalize a culture of customer service, on-time delivery, high quality, and results-oriented performance.

6. Reward IT executives and managers on their outcomes that drive business value at all levels.

Lutchen's book contains more than timely advice for the modern CIO—it's a road map for IT suppliers trying to get inside the minds of their customers. Here's something to consider: If the CIO's goal is linking IT strategy to corporate strategy, shouldn't you be doing everything possible to help the CIO achieve that goal?

If you look carefully, you'll find that each supplier in the CIO's "inner circle" is actively and energetically helping the CIO align the IT organization with the rest of the enterprise.

Points Along the Curve

We all have a tendency to generalize, especially when we're trying to construct a good argument. But here's a thought

Aligning with the CIO's Objectives

CIO Responsibilities	How the Vendor Can Help
Align IT operations with enterprise business goals.	Consider the impact of any proposed solution on the larger enterprise.
Manage IT as a business.	Look beyond your annual objectives and understand that the CIO is looking at the long-term view (5-7 years).
Link IT strategy with corporate strategy.	Make sure you understand how the needs of individual business units map to the objectives of the larger enterprise.
Identify and prioritize business needs across the enterprise.	Respect IT governance; document business needs and recommendations *without* the use of exasperating sales jargon.
Satisfy internal and external business clients.	Put skin in the game; don't walk away after the contract is signed; deliver on your promises.
Drive business value.	Measure success; show the client how your project delivered value over time.

Figure 1.1 CIOs want to work with suppliers who understand their objectives and align their sales tactics accordingly.

worth remembering: There is no "standard" CIO. Each CIO is unique. Each brings a slightly different set of skills to the job—and each CIO operates within his or her own personal comfort zone.

Don't expect every CIO to be

- A whiz at financial analysis.

- A management genius.

- Familiar with the latest technologies.

- Capable of envisioning the enterprise-wide consequences of his or her purchasing decisions.

Every CIO is likely to benefit from some measure of your insight, guidance, and advice. It's your job to determine how much help the CIO needs—and to provide that help in a way the CIO finds palatable.

Chapter TWO

IT Is a Business

"My number one responsibility is bringing financial transparency to the IT organization. My job is taking this big black hole of IT expense and putting it in a cost accounting framework."

Mike Blake

Senior Vice President of
IT Finance, First Data

Show Me the Cost Structure

The problem with many IT sales reps is that they think mainly in terms of making deals.

"The minute you're walking in the door, you're talking about the deal," laments Mark Lutchen. "But that's not what IT is about anymore. First, you have to show me the cost structure. You have to pull together the information I would need to make a business case for your product. Then we can talk about a deal."

Lutchen's pointed advice underscores just how much the IT function has changed over the past 35 years. Contrary to popular belief, early IT managers weren't any more logical or disciplined than any other group of managers at the time. They just seemed smarter and brighter than everyone else because they worked with computers.

As a group, today's IT executives are really and truly bright people. Well educated and well traveled, they have interests outside of IT. They know that they're living in a global economy that's driven by information. They think of themselves as businesspeople.

And they think of IT as a business, not as a function.

When you visit with an IT executive today, it's not un-usual to see a copy of Thomas L. Friedman's *The World Is Flat* sitting on the bookshelf, along with books about lead-ership, management, economics, finance, and accounting. You may see a book about programming tucked away in a corner.

IT executives see themselves managing technology to drive shareholder value, not for technology's sake. *Managing IT as a Business* lists seven drivers of shareholder value guiding today's executives:

1. Revenue and earnings growth

2. Capital spending

3. New distribution channels

4. Cash flow management

5. Cost reduction

6. R&D/innovation

7. Marketing/advertising

As an IT supplier, you should commit these seven drivers to memory. Think of them as foundational elements of every IT deal.

Each deal, of course, will have its own unique mix of driv-ers. No single formula is guaranteed to work in all situations.

But you can ratchet down the level of uncertainty and improve your chances of success by using the seven drivers as your starting point.

For example, let's say that you're selling a CRM solution and your primary business sponsor is the vice president of customer acquisition. It's obvious that revenue growth will be this person's top driver. Because you're an experienced sales rep, you'll keep the conversations focused on all the nifty ways your solution will boost the customer's top line.

But it would be a mistake to stop there. Cost reduction will also be an important driver for this vice president, since he or she will be held accountable for managing customer acquisition costs, which in turn will be connected to marketing/advertising, another driver.

New distribution channels will be an additional driver for this vice president, since many of the new customers he or she hopes to acquire can be reached through wireless telephony or the Web.

New distribution channels will require the vice president's company to invent new and unique ways to differentiate customer interactions, which affect yet another driver, R&D/innovation.

Let's pick another technology area where we can apply Lutchen's list of seven drivers. If you're selling a supplier rationalization project, your primary sponsor will be the vice president of procurement. Supplier rationalization projects are designed primarily to lower a company's overall costs and reduce capital spending, often by shrinking the number of suppliers required to fulfill the company's needs.

One-time cost savings are rarely the goal of such projects. Instead, the goal is building solid relationships with key suppliers that continually reduce costs and improve performance.

The vice president of procurement also will be looking for innovative methods for achieving higher levels of efficiency, since it's a sure bet that their department is already stretched thin.

Greater efficiency, along with improved consistency of performance, will enable the vice president to make better forecasts and predictions, leading to more accurate budget plans. Greater accuracy in budget planning usually leads to improved cash flow management and increased earning growth.

With a modest amount of effort and a few hours of additional research, you can easily weave three or four of the seven drivers into every sales presentation.

Connecting All the Dots

CIOs appreciate the value of a well written business case—but only when it's relevant to their business.

"The worst thing a sales person can do is come in with a cookie cutter value proposition," says Avi Halutz, vice president of technology at Time Inc. "A business case needs to be relevant to my organization's business issues. It can't be some generic document whipped up by the vendor's marketing department."

Developing a Solid Business Case

Many of the CIOs we interviewed told us stories about sitting through business case presentations that were largely irrelevant to their specific business challenges.

Several years ago, it would have been okay to assume that a business case written about a company within an industry in one vertical would be relevant to a prospect at another company in the same vertical.

It is no longer safe to make that assumption. Today, any business case that you present must be directly relevant to the target audience. For example, if you're selling to a manufacturer, the business case that you present should be directly relevant to the experiences of that manufacturer.

A well written business case recently helped a sales account team at SAS Institute win a major contract and deepen its relationship with a client. Here's the story in brief.

In mid-2004, a major telecom decided that it needed a large-scale CRM solution and approached several IT suppliers with an RFP (request for proposal). As the suppliers responded to the RFP, it became apparent that the cost of a large implementation would be an insurmountable hurdle. So the telecom decided to scale down the project.

The field of competitors quickly narrowed to SAS and another supplier. SAS decided to differentiate itself by developing a detailed business case analysis that clearly defined the value of its product suite.

The sales account team determined that a strong business case would be an important element of the pre-sales and post-sales phases of the project. The business case process itself would also serve as a forum for keeping everyone focused on solving the client's immediate business challenges.

The account team relied on an internal business analyst, Lloyd Lyons, and an outside marketing consultant, Shaun Doyle of Cognitive Box, to write the business case. The account team also developed a financial summary to help the client visualize the results of its investment. The summary included the following:

- *A five-year profit and loss analysis.*
- *ROI (return on investment) calculation.*
- *Payback period.*
- *NPV (net present value), using the customer's weighted average cost of capital.*
- *Monthly cost of delaying the project by one month.*
- *Impact on the customer financial statements, including annual increase in revenue (steady-state); annual increase in operating income (steady-state); recent market capitalization and increase in market capitalization;*

recent share price; increase in share price and improve-ment in share price.

As members of the account team gathered data for the business case, an unexpected benefit emerged: They made valuable new contacts with key decision makers and influencers within the client's organization, deepening and extending their relationships with the client.

Early drafts of the business case were shared with the client's marketing team, which enabled the account team to build crucial relationships with key sponsors of the project. The client's CMO and CIO took part in editing the business case, which created a sense of partnership that proved invaluable as the sales effort progressed.

The final version of the business case was used by the project's internal sponsors to justify the company's investment and to monitor delivery of the project. In the end, the business case allowed the sales account team to engage more deeply with key players at the client's organization, including the CMO, CIO, and CFO. They, along with others, emerged as champions for the project.

Today, the business case continues to serve as a road map for guiding higher-level decisions in the implementation process. It also provides a template for monitoring the success of the project and for tracking the shareholder value it generates for the client.

Most important, from the sales perspective, the business case is a foundation for continuing efforts by the sales account team to deepen its relationship with the client.

New Faces, Old Issues

Despite their sophistication and worldly knowledge, many of today's IT managers spend an enormous amount of their time solving problems created by their predecessors.

Lacking formal business training, early IT managers rarely created formal processes for managing their IT assets. As a result, Lutchen writes, "Many companies simply do not know in any sort of detail or with any accuracy what IT assets they own, where those assets reside, and how much it costs to run them on an ongoing basis."

However, not all of the problems associated with legacy IT infrastructure can be traced to poor decisions made by a previous generation of IT managers. As Lutchen correctly observes, "Business-unit executives often implement technology solutions to address various business issues without in any way projecting the ongoing costs of maintaining those systems."

The "spaghetti of legacy IT infrastructure," as Lutchen humorously describes it, provides ripe opportunities for IT suppliers with solutions engineered to replace or augment older technology. But don't expect today's IT buyers to take your word for it.

The Vice President of Transparency

When you're selling IT to a big company such as First Data Corporation, you will meet lots and lots of people. But you might never meet Mike Blake.

Mike Blake is the senior vice president of IT finance at First Data. Companies such as First Data are increasingly hiring people like Mike Blake to ride herd over their IT spending.

But Blake wasn't hired to cut costs. He was hired to measure value. Blake represents a new breed of IT executive: the techie with a degree in finance.

"My number one responsibility is bringing financial transparency to the IT organization," Blake explains. "My job is taking this big black hole of IT expense and putting it in a cost accounting framework."

Blake is a certified public accountant. He also holds an MBA from the University of Chicago School of Business. For Blake, real transparency begins with good accounting.

Once you've agreed to approach IT spending with the mind-set of an accountant, it immediately becomes easier to identify the true costs of specific applications and services within your IT portfolio.

"Sometimes this transparency stuff can be pretty scary," he admits. "Not all people are comfortable with transparency. It's like taking your shirt off in public. Suddenly you don't look so good anymore. When you have IT transparency, you find out which apps are consuming your resources. It can really surprise you."

Blake remembers a situation that occurred several years back, at another company. "We retired a fleet of applications. But our cost accounting system was still showing costs. At first we just assumed the cost accounting system must be wrong. The deeper we looked, the more bizarre it got. Eventually we discovered that not all the apps had been retired."

Several of the retired apps were still running, at a cost to the company of about $300,000 a month!

"The infrastructure guy didn't look good, because he didn't know what was running on his infrastructure," says Blake. "The CTO didn't look good, because he declared the apps dead. And the CIO had egg on his face because he believed what his guys were telling him, and then spent four months blaming the cost accounting system."

The situation embarrassed the IT department, and taught everyone an expensive lesson about the value of transparency. Faced with cold, hard financial facts, they quickly off-loaded the operations to a less expensive alternative.

Worst of all, recalls Blake, the vendor said nothing. "At what point should the vendor have said something? At what point does the vendor become accountable? When should the vendor say, 'Hey, you're doing something stupid, I can show you a better, less expensive way to do this'?"

How Suppliers Benefit from IT Transparency

For Blake, transparency is a two-way street with clear benefits for IT organizations and their suppliers. For IT organizations, transparency translates into a greater awareness of which apps or services are providing real value and which aren't. That awareness, ideally, results in better management of resources.

On the sell side, transparency makes it easier for suppliers to prove the business value of the products or services they sell. Transparency also creates opportunities for an agile supplier by revealing gaps in a customer's IT portfolio that, presumably, the supplier can fill.

Smart IT suppliers will put transparency to work for them by pitching services and products that they know will generate measurable and unambiguous business value. Transparency enables IT suppliers to position themselves as strategic partners of the CIO.

When asked to describe a pitch from a supplier who knows how to leverage transparency, Blake offered a hypothetical scenario:

> *A supplier we trust comes in and tells us that we're wasting lots of money on a legacy app with a clunky interface that's sucking up all kinds of processing time. He tells us that his company can save us x-number of dollars over the next x-number of years if we port over to another language and hire freelance talent to write the code.*

"It's that simple," says Blake. "You don't need a huge consulting firm to accomplish this. You just need a couple of smart people and some programmers."

Suppliers waste less time when selling to transparent organizations because the numbers they need to build credible business cases are readily available.

Transparency also makes it easier for IT organizations and suppliers to launch CPFR (collaborative planning, forecasting, and replenishment) initiatives. "If the IT organization can provide accurate forecasts of its needs over the next 18 to 24 months, the supplier can figure out a way to reduce costs and pass the savings along," explains Blake. "Then everybody's happy."

Let's Define Our Terms

Since the natural language of business is finance and the corporate IT department functions more like a business unit than a service center, business-oriented CIOs have become increasingly fluent in the language of finance.

That puts the technology-focused sales rep at a distinct disadvantage. Every day, the CIO becomes more immersed in the grammar and syntax of finance. If this trend continues, it will be difficult for an IT sales rep to engage the CIO in a truly meaningful dialogue—unless the sales rep has a grounding in finance.

It seems logical, therefore, that IT sales reps who want to develop and maintain long-term business relationships with CIOs need to hit the books. If you don't know the basics of corporate finance, sign up for a course at the nearest college. Most colleges will let you audit classes for a reduced charge. We guarantee that you will be pleasantly surprised at how valuable taking an introductory finance course will be to your career and to your life. Look at Figures 2.1 and 2.2.

Growing the Installed Base

IT organizations that are truly committed to financial transparency actually make life easier for suppliers by providing them with the proof they need to show that their products or services are delivering genuine value.

Let's take a moment to consider this idea. A mere 20 years ago, the notion that IT vendors were responsible for delivering value to their customers would have seemed completely misguided. Back in the 1980s, everybody knew that IT vendors existed to sell IT products.

Today we can agree that delivering value is not just a supplier's responsibility; it's the single most important factor in determining any supplier's long-term success in the marketplace.

For an IT supplier, there are two prerequisites for maintaining stable relationships with customers: the ability to

Financial Terms Associated with Making a Purchase Decision

Capital Budgeting: The process when management must allocate limited resources between competing opportunities ("projects"). In general, each project's value will be estimated using a discounted cash flow (DCF) valuation.

Capital Expense: A capital expenditure is one that will benefit one year or more. It can increase the quantity or quality of services to be gained from the asset. It is charged to an asset account.

Cost of Capital: A weighted sum of the minimum rate of return a firm must offer shareholders and the cost of debt.

Cost of Goods Sold (COGS): Describes the direct expenses incurred in producing a particular good for sale, including the actual cost of materials that comprise the good, and direct labor expense in putting the good in salable condition.

Discounted Cash Flows: An approach describes a method to value a project or an entire company. The DCF methods determine the present value of future cash flows by discounting them using the appropriate cost of capital.

Earnings per Share (EPS): The earnings returned on the initial investment amount. You calculate earnings per share by taking the net earnings and dividing by the outstanding shares. Trailing EPS = last year's numbers (Actual). Current EPS = this year's numbers (Projection). Forward EPS = future numbers (Projection).

Gross Margin: Expresses the relationship between gross profit and sales revenue. The ambiguity arises because it can be expressed in absolute terms: Gross Margin = Revenue − Cost of Goods Sold.

Hurdle Rate: The minimum expected return a company will consider in accepting investment opportunities.

Figure 2.1 As relationships between CFOs and CIOs become more closely interwoven, it's crucial for IT suppliers to master the language of finance.

Source: Thomas Friedel and others.

**Financial Terms Associated
with Making a Purchase Decision**

Internal Rate of Return (IRR): A capital budgeting method used by firms to decide whether they should make long-term investments. The IRR is the return rate that can be earned on the invested capital, that is the yield on the investment.

Net Income (Bottom Line): Income that a firm has after subtracting costs and expenses from the total revenue. Net income is sometimes called the bottom line because it is typically found on the last line of a company's income statement.

Net Present Value (NPV): A standard method for financial evaluation of long-term projects. Present value of cash inflows– Present value of cash outflows (or minus initial investment in most of the cases).

Operating Income: A measure of a company's earning power from ongoing operations, equal to earnings before deduction of interest payments and income taxes. Also called operating profit or EBIT (earnings before interest and taxes).

Payback Period: The period of time required for the return on an investment to "repay" the sum of the original investment.

Revenues (Top Line): An income term, referring to the money owed the company for sales of goods and services.

Selling, General, and Administrative Expenses (SG&A): An income statement category, for costs not linked to the production of specific goods, including all selling, general company expense, and expenses.

Shareholder Value: Primary goal for a company is to enrich its shareholders (owners) by paying dividends and/or causing the stock price to increase.

Total Cost of Ownership: The total cost of acquiring, installing, using, maintaining, changing, and getting rid of something across an extended period of time (most or all of its useful life).

Figure 2.2 Today's detailed business cases require more than vague references to increased revenue and lower costs.
Source: Thomas Friedel and others.

deliver value and the ability to prove that value is being delivered.

Stable relationships, in turn, are essential for expanding an IT supplier's installed base. The supplier with the largest installed base has an advantage that's hard to beat.

Resist the urge to measure the size of your installed base by totaling up the number of user licenses you've sold. Instead, measure your installed base by calculating the value created by the users for their organizations.

Just because you sell a bunch of seats doesn't mean people are using your software. Think about that for a few moments. You made the sale, but nobody's using the stuff you sold. How will you get customer references? What will the industry analysts write or say about your products?

Worst of all, your customers will be angry and upset because you sold them products they didn't really need. How do you think the CIOs of those organizations will feel about doing business with you again?

And even if you manage to get those CIOs on the phone again, do you really believe that their CFOs or CEOs will forget that your company sold them products they didn't use?

If you're seeking an example to support this argument, you don't have to look further back in time than the late 1990s, when bad word-of-mouth came dangerously close to ruining the market for CRM software. In the case of CRM, a few early implementation fiascos nearly destroyed an entire class of products. It took years for CRM software to reenter the mainstream.

Can You Do the Right Thing?

Time and again, CIOs told us how impressed they would be if IT suppliers had the courage to pull the plug on projects that were going nowhere.

Sure, it would take guts. And no doubt, there would be short-term pain to cope with. The alternative—saying nothing—might appear the easier and wiser course. But consider the trade-off: Your silence today guarantees an ugly scene tomorrow when the customer realizes that you haven't delivered on your promises. If your goal is building long-term, profitable relationships with your customers, then honesty is the best policy.

After all, when analysts rank vendors, they're looking at execution. To say that a vendor is innovative is a nice compliment, but what CIOs really want to know is whether the vendor's products work as advertised.

An IT supplier with its eye on the future encourages and supports the efforts of its sales force to go beyond the transaction. Truly visionary IT suppliers create real incentives for sales reps who walk the extra mile to ensure that the products they sell are properly deployed and utilized to create value for their customers.

IT and Shareholder Value

As mentioned in the previous chapter, IT has evolved beyond its original boundaries.

"In the past," says Paul Zazzera, "IT was all about making the payroll process go faster or reducing labor costs. Today, Wal-Mart and other innovative companies are teaching us that IT can be used to expand a business dramatically."

Now the role of IT is very closely connected to the concept of shareholder value. That means that CIOs don't spend all of their time trying to reduce costs—they spend most of their time figuring out how to grow the business.

That's a huge difference in perspective. Today, the people who make purchasing decisions about IT still read plenty of technical publications, but they also read *Fortune*, *BusinessWeek*, and the *Wall Street Journal*. They understand their company's position in the market, and they care deeply about the performance of its stock.

"Wall Street looks for predictable growth," says Zazzera. "So if you are selling to me, you have to tell me how your product or service is going to improve my bottom line. You have to explain how the $10 million you want me to spend with your company will generate $100 million in value for my company."

In an environment where steady growth and increasing profitability are highly prized, it's an uphill battle to sell IT purely on the basis of cost savings.

"Sure, you can talk about how much money you're going to save my company or how much more efficient your product will make our operations," says Zazzera. "Cost savings matter, but at the end of the day what counts is shareholder value. What I really want to know from you is: Will this investment deliver a solid return?"

Eight out of ten times, says Zazzera, that question is enough to derail an IT vendor's sales pitch. "A good sales rep can talk to rocks. But that question usually slows the conversation."

The CIOs we interviewed uniformly agreed that many sales reps are not fully prepared or trained to discuss the multiyear financial impact of what they're selling, and that relatively few sales reps are capable of articulating the value proposition in terms that are meaningful or relevant to the customer.

"You have to make me believe that you're going to add value," says Zazzera. "That means you need to know our industry, our company, and understand our business issues well enough to speak in the same language I'm speaking."

Perfect Pitch?

When we interviewed IT executives for this book, we asked them to describe an ideal pitch. Zazzera's answer to our question was typical of the responses:

Explain the value proposition very clearly. Show us how you're going to help us improve our top line and our bottom line. Have a referenceable portfolio. Show us that you can be comfortable in conversations with the COO or the CEO. Be prepared to offer a strong business argument in language that top executives can easily understand.

In a perfect world, every sales pitch would include a detailed financial model showing the internal rate of return (IRR), the net present value (NPV), and the economic value added (EVA) of the proposed capital expenditure.

In that same perfect world, the CIO would know the hurdle rate, or required rate of return, above which an investment would make sense and below which it would not.

These are complex financial concepts that most sales reps are not comfortable chatting about in the course of a standard sales pitch. And the truth is that many CIOs aren't going to feel comfortable chatting about them, either.

But here's the reality: Sooner or later, the CIO's boss or the steering committee that approves the CIO's budget, or the company's board of directors, is going to ask for detailed calculations showing the expected financial impact of the proposed purchase. At that point, both the CIO and the supplier had better be ready with some credible estimates, preferably expressed in the language of finance.

After all, we're not talking about nickels and dimes. In a single year, a large corporation can easily spend hundreds of millions of dollars on IT. Some global organizations already spend more than $1 billion annually on IT.

With numbers that large, it should come as no surprise that prospective buyers are demanding stronger and more precise business arguments from suppliers before finalizing deals.

Money Doesn't Grow on Trees

Sadly, many suppliers just don't understand the modern CIO's predicament. Almost every CIO we interviewed told stories about suppliers who apparently believe that in addition to its other responsibilities, the IT department also prints money.

Unless new funds are allocated, the CIO can spend only what's already in the IT budget. The only way the CIO can find money for an unbudgeted project is to take money away from a project that's already been given the green light.

Barring a crisis or disaster, the CIO is not likely to press for a last-minute reallocation of funds. What's more likely is that the CIO will be pressured to trim or cut funding for existing projects. That's the reality!

Let's pause for a moment to validate your gut feeling that IT sales hasn't turned out to be the cushy career choice you thought it would be.

Indeed, a quick stroll through a hypothetical version of a typical IT budgeting scenario reveals hazards for the IT supplier lurking at every turn.

1. An IT supplier helps a business unit within a company identify a need. The supplier helps the business unit develop an initiative to address the need. The initiative will be forwarded to the company's IT department for consideration.

2. IT reviews the initiative and figures out what it should cost. Sometimes IT seeks estimates or advice from other suppliers. IT sends its cost estimate back to the business unit.

3. The business unit decides whether it can afford the cost of the initiative. If the cost is too high, the business might abandon the initiative, modify it, or work with the supplier to lower the cost.

4. If the cost is something the business unit can live with, and if IT determines the project is feasible, the initiative is included in a draft version of the IT budget.

5. The budget draft is reviewed by the steering committee, who are also considering initiatives from every

business unit within the company. Responding to pressure from the CEO, the committee mandates 20 percent cost reductions for each new project. Now it's back to the drawing board.

6. A revised budget for the initiative is approved, but spending for new projects is frozen a month later when the company doesn't hit its numbers.

At this point in our hypothetical scenario, the CIO calls the supplier and explains that the initiative will be delayed. The supplier responds by offering to drop the price another 10 percent. When the CIO explains that all funding for new projects has been frozen, the supplier drops the price another 5 percent.

The supplier just doesn't get it: If there isn't any money for the project in the IT budget, the CIO is powerless. Additional discounts won't help. The supplier can only hope that the CIO's company will hit its numbers soon and that the steering committee will restore financing for the project.

"When stuff like that happens, it's not my fault and it's not the vendor's fault. It's just the dynamics of business. Some people are invariably disappointed," observes Zazzera.

Here's a real-world example of the hard circumstances facing IT suppliers and their customers:

Until recently, most companies replaced their PCs every three years, based on IRS depreciation schedules. It didn't matter whether the PCs were working or broken; they were replaced with newer models. The PC manufacturers counted on selling those replacement PCs when forecasting their revenues. For them, it was like money in the bank.

Then a fresh wave of cost cutting swept across the corporate landscape. Companies decided they could wait another year before replacing their PCs. Their three-year depreciation cycle suddenly became a four-year depreciation cycle. Overnight, PC makers who were hailed as visionary geniuses in the late 1990s found themselves described as myopic and dysfunctional. Many of the PC makers still haven't entirely recovered—and some never will.

"Hey, it's difficult to be a vendor in the IT industry right now," says Zazzera. "It's not like the old days. Today you have to demonstrate value. Money doesn't grow on trees, right?"

Guess Again

In some industries, it's possible to guess the size of a company's IT budget by looking at its overall spending, but in other industries, your rule of thumb estimate would be way off the mark. For example, the cruise industry traditionally allocates large sums of money to build and maintain ships, but those spending levels don't translate into boundless funds for IT. (See Figure 2.3.)

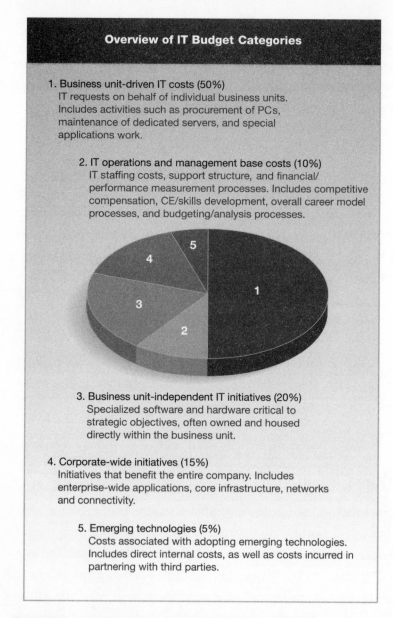

Overview of IT Budget Categories

1. Business unit-driven IT costs (50%)
   IT requests on behalf of individual business units.
   Includes activities such as procurement of PCs,
   maintenance of dedicated servers, and special
   applications work.

2. IT operations and management base costs (10%)
   IT staffing costs, support structure, and financial/
   performance measurement processes. Includes competitive
   compensation, CE/skills development, overall career model
   processes, and budgeting/analysis processes.

3. Business unit-independent IT initiatives (20%)
   Specialized software and hardware critical to
   strategic objectives, often owned and housed
   directly within the business unit.

4. Corporate-wide initiatives (15%)
   Initiatives that benefit the entire company. Includes
   enterprise-wide applications, core infrastructure, networks
   and connectivity.

5. Emerging technologies (5%)
   Costs associated with adopting emerging technologies.
   Includes direct internal costs, as well as costs incurred in
   partnering with third parties.

Figure 2.3 Here's how a typical IT budget is divided. Where do your products and services fit in this chart?
Source: Adapted from Mark Lutchen.

Myles Cyr, vice president and CIO of Carnival Cruise Lines, recalls when a solutions vendor dropped a huge proposal on his desk. The vendor, which primarily sold products to clients in another industry, was surprised by Cyr's lack of interest in pursuing a deal.

"In certain sectors of the economy, companies will drop millions on IT solutions without blinking, but you can't knock on my door expecting the same thing," says Cyr. "When sales reps call on us, it's important for them to understand how our spending priorities differ from those of the last customer they called on. We're different from other industries, and I expect sales reps to bring specific knowledge of our priorities to the table."

This is especially relevant when calling on prospects in the public sector. Applying sales tactics that might work successfully in many parts of the private sector would be inappropriate in most parts of the public sector.

Marcia Bohannon, CIO of Jeffco Public Schools in Golden, Colorado, says some vendors try to create a false sense of urgency in their quest to close deals and make quotas. This tactic rarely works in the public sector, she says.

"In the public sector, our budget is set way in advance," notes Bohannon. "One of my pet peeves is when a vendor thinks our budget cycle mirrors its annual sales year. We have our own calendar, and our own priorities. We have a lot of limitations on what we can spend."

Chapter THREE

Delivery

"Do your homework and don't rush a deal through the process. Rushing can cause problems down the road—and clients hate surprises."

Gary Fink
Partner, Accenture

Delivery Is Everything

You won't grow your revenue year over year if you can't keep your customers happy. And you won't keep your customers happy unless you consistently deliver on your promises. It's a pretty simple equation.

Despite its outward simplicity, it's an equation that many vendors find difficult to solve. Even today, after all the philosophizing and speechifying about the importance of "customer-centricity," many vendors remain fixated on their products. They ignore or forget about their customers because they actually believe that their products are more important than the customers using them!

Blinded by their "product-centricity," these vendors don't have a clue. And they don't even care—until they run out of money and go looking for investors to replenish their hoard of cash.

But when they sit down for a meeting with venture capitalists or investment bankers, here are the first two questions they hear:

1. Is your R&D solid?

2. Are your customers happy?

Perhaps not coincidentally, those also are questions asked by CIOs when they're considering investing in an IT vendor's product or service.

Like professional investors, CIOs aren't likely to believe everything they read on your web site about your latest, greatest product. If they're truly interested, they'll pick up the phone and call around until they find a CIO who is already using the product. Then they'll get the real scoop. If you've kept your promises to the client, they'll hear good things about you. If you haven't kept your promises—well, you can imagine what they'll hear.

Decision makers like John von Stein, EVP and CIO of Options Clearing Corporation want to know how a vendor is perceived by its customers. "Knowing how many widgets a vendor sold is of no value when making a decision," says von Stein. "I want to know how many of their customers are seeing the value that was promised to them."

Von Stein's due diligence goes far beyond making a few reference calls or reading a couple of case studies sent over by a vendor. Like other CIOs, he picks up the phone and calls his peers for a reality check.

He also structures deals that start with a "pass or fail" proof step. "We can't afford to make a mistake when picking a strategic supplier. The risk is not just about wasting the development costs—it's the switching costs that are worrisome. Once you pick a vendor, you're embedded with them in a way that makes it somewhat cost prohibitive to make a change," he explains.

Keep Your Promises

Like all other consumers, CIOs suffer buyer's remorse. Before the ink on the contract is dry, they begin wondering if they made the right choice. They begin worrying about whether you will deliver on your promises.

Their greatest fear is that after the deal is done and the sale is completed, your product will not perform as advertised. Yes, they've got your obligations written into the contract eight ways from Sunday. But all those legal niceties don't matter to the CIO. After the contract is signed, all the CIO really cares about it is this: Will it work?

We're not making this up. This is a fact that you need to know, whether you're part of the account team or a consultant. A key question rolling through the mind of every CIO is: What happens after the sale?

So if you believe that delivery is someone else's problem, we're here to tell you that the CIO believes differently. The CIO believes that it's *your* problem.

A survey conducted by *CIO* magazine in 2006 shows that of the 10 vendor attributes considered most important by CIOs, the ability to deliver on promises ranks number one. (See Figure 3.1.)

"96 percent of respondents chose 'vendor delivers on promises' as the most important vendor attribute," says Michael Friedenberg, CEO of the magazine's parent firm, CXO Media, "but only 54 percent agreed that vendors keep their promises. That's a huge gap."

The survey results also showed significant gaps between the expectations of CIOs and their perceptions about how well vendors were meeting those expectations. For example, 93 percent of the survey's respondents said it was crucial for vendors to meet deadlines and set realistic schedules, but only 50 percent believed that vendors actually met deadlines and set realistic schedules.

Another example: 93 percent of respondents said it was important for vendors to provide ongoing support through the post-sales phase, but only 54 percent said that vendors were providing such support.

"We found tremendous gaps," says Friedenberg. The survey also revealed "that CIOs won't recommend a vendor unless the vendor lives up to its promises." That's an absolutely essential piece of intelligence for vendors: If you don't live up to your promises, CIOs will not recommend you to their peers.

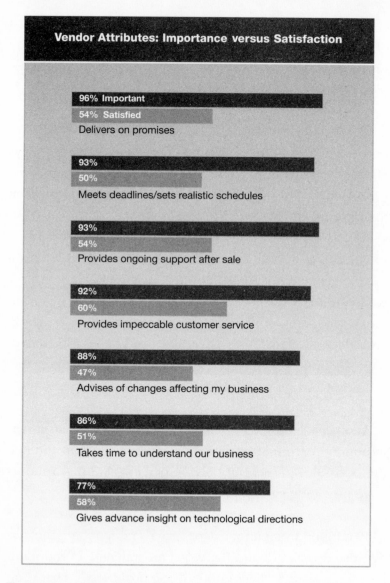

Figure 3.1 This survey shows clearly which vendor attributes are considered crucial by CIOs and where vendors are falling short.

Source: Adapted from *CIO* magazine research project, "The Role and Influence of the 21st Century CIO."

Now consider this: CIOs typically rate peer recommendations as critical factors in their purchasing decisions. And CIOs talk to other CIOs—frequently.

In many respects, the IT industry is like a small village. Bad news spreads quickly. If you or your organization foul up, everyone knows. CIOs tend to have long memories. If you wrong them, they'll take their sense of grievance with them to the grave. That's a compelling argument for keeping your promises.

The best way to ensure that all your promises are kept is by making a conscious effort to stay involved with the client after the sale. Staying involved after the sale has several benefits:

- The more involved you remain, the more you increase the odds of satisfying your client's expectations.

- Successful implementations will earn you the peer recommendations that are essential for winning new clients.

- Good word of mouth from clients generates favorable PR and positive analyst coverage that moves you up the Magic Quadrant.

- Satisfied clients are more likely to request your involvement in other projects or recommend you to others within their organization.

- IT suppliers who keep their promises are invited into the CIO's inner circle.

Feeling Disconnected?

IT suppliers like to talk about product integration, but they also need to arrive at the table with an integrated team of players who are fully invested in the success of the project.

Many of our sources referred to the unpleasant sense of disconnection they experience when speaking with people from different parts of a vendor's organization.

You might think, "Gee, that's too bad, but it's really not my problem if a client feels a sense of disconnection when dealing with other parts of my organization. Sorry, there's nothing I can do."

In the delivery phase of a project, this kind of thinking can prove fatal to your career. Here's why: All of your sales and marketing materials promote your organization as a seamlessly integrated technology provider. All of your sales presentations emphasize the end-to-end capabilities of your organization's products and services. You've probably used the word "holistic" at least a hundred times in conversations with the client.

If your organization messes up the delivery phase and you fail to do anything to rectify the problem, it becomes apparent to the client that your organization is not end-to-end, not integrated, and not holistic. It becomes apparent to the client that you've been exaggerating the seamless quality of your organization and overstating your ability to influence the various parts of your organization required to pull off an implementation.

Suddenly your organization is revealed for what it is—a loose collection of disparate pieces held together by a corporate logo. There's a word for this: "dysfunctional."

Sometimes an IT vendor's dysfunctionality extends to encompass its consulting partners. The consultant thinks the account team cares only about making its sales quota, and the account team think the consultant cares only about making a profit. Each blames the other when a problem arises.

Lack of cooperation between a vendor's account team and its consulting partners is not uncommon, but it's always unwelcome. If the tension is excruciatingly obvious, the deal can fall apart. Then all of your hard work selling the project will amount to nothing.

Don't turn your internal issues into the customer's problem. Your issues should be resolved before you come to the table—and they should be invisible to the client.

Consistently successful IT suppliers make certain that all the components of their sales and delivery teams work together throughout the various phases of a project. Successful IT suppliers know that clients don't think about pre-sales and post-sales. Above all, successful IT suppliers understand that the sale isn't complete until the client is satisfied.

"Sometimes salespeople are under extraordinary pressure to accomplish their personal goals, so they get myopic. They don't understand that until there's successful implementation, you won't have a happy customer—and you won't get repeat business," says Alec Palmer, CIO of the Federal Election Commission.

Seeing Through the Client's Eyes

"Account teams often focus on the day-to-day tactical progress of a project," observes Gary Fink, a veteran consulting executive in Accenture's Financial Services operating group. "But you need to stay focused on the client's business issue—that's the reason you were hired in the first place."

That means seeing the project through the client's eyes, understanding their vision and knowing how they define success. "The bells and whistles you deliver along the way will be seen as insignificant unless the client sees that you have helped solve the problem or leveraged an opportunity," says Fink.

He acknowledges that employee turnover—both on the sales side and on the client side—can make it easy to lose sight of the big picture. You can avoid this by helping the client define and document their vision at the outset of the project, and then by carefully measuring progress as the project proceeds.

"Make sure that you understand the complexities before the project is initiated," he recommends. "Do your homework and don't rush a deal through the process. Rushing can cause problems down the road—and clients hate surprises. If you come back to the table again and again with new information and explanations, trust will be lost, and clients may think that you're more focused on selling than helping them."

Avoid blaming problems on existing processes or technologies that your solution or service was supposed to work with. Continual alignment of expectations is critical to building your relationship with the client and to helping solve the problem your products and/or services were purchased to address.

"You are your client's trusted advisor," says Fink. "Don't wait until the last minute to pull in your technicians and product specialists. Clients want to know the 'how to' a lot earlier than you may think. Make the implementers a transparent part of your account team, which will ensure a smooth transition into post-sales."

If you think things are not going well, don't hesitate to throw a red flag. Clients prefer honesty to surprises, and they'll appreciate getting a heads up sooner rather than later. Whatever you do, don't disappear after the contract is signed. Stay visible and stay involved.

Don't Forget about Your Client's Brand

When companies choose your IT products or services, they're staking their reputations on your ability to deliver. They entrust you with their brands. Their customers aren't aware that you, the IT supplier, provide the back end solution that fills their prescriptions or keeps track of their stock trades.

Third Party Solutions of Memphis, Tennessee, for example, is the nation's largest provider of workers' compensation prescription programs. Its customers include pharmacy chains, grocery store chains, mass merchant chains, and independent pharmacies in every state.

The company also provides a 24/7 online claims processing network supported by a sophisticated computer system and a call center staffed by specially trained personnel. Anything less than 100 percent uptime would result in lost business for clients who depend on Third Party Solutions to provide the IT resources necessary for processing millions of pharmacy claims quickly and accurately.

As a back end IT services supplier, Third Party Solutions is invisible to consumers, but the quality and consistency of its performance directly affect the brand reputations of its clients. Any glitch or interruption of service to a client can result in lost customers and damaged reputations.

One way or another, every IT supplier plays a vital role in maintaining the brand reputations of its clients. Sometimes it's easy to forget that the CIO is rarely the end user.

Be Up Front about Implementation Requirements

Michelle Garvey, the CIO of Warnaco, speaks for CIOs worldwide when she says: "I don't like surprises." She urges vendors to be up front when additional services or extra modules are required for a fully successful deployment. Garvey still bristles when recalling an incident at a previous job in which a sales force automation vendor tried selling her software without the services necessary to get it up and running. "They knew we couldn't do it on our own. They were going to wait and then sell us a 100-hour pack of support services. I don't like finding out that I need to buy something after I've done a deal."

Like Gary Fink, she understands that tensions arise between IT vendors and their consulting partners. "But they have to understand that I am looking for a solution. They need to work together."

Even when the account team and the implementation team work for the same company, internal disagreements over revenue and profit can impede a project. Garvey offers this advice to vendors: "Solve your problems. I don't care how you do it. You know what I need. Make it happen."

"How'm I doin'?"

Ed Koch, the outspoken mayor of New York City from 1978 to 1989, used to greet his fellow New Yorkers with a wave and a question: "How'm I doin'?" Koch was legendary for his blunt honesty. Some adored him for it; others loathed him for it. "How'm I doin'?" was his signature phrase, his way of reminding citizens that he cared.

It wouldn't be a bad idea for IT suppliers to adopt similar phrases and include them in their communications with clients, especially in the delivery phase of a project.

Gregory S. Smith, vice president and CIO of Information Technology at the World Wildlife Fund (WWF) in Washington, D.C. and the author of *Straight to the Top: Becoming a World-Class CIO*, has formalized the post-sales communications process with a four-part vendor survey that serves as a sort of self-evaluation.

Each year, Smith and his team select a group of vendors to complete the form, which includes both qualitative and quantitative questions, of which 10 are related directly to performance. The 10 questions ask the vendors to grade their performance in a variety of areas. We applaud Smith's creativity, and we're happy that he's agreed to share the list of questions with us.

"IT has become more pragmatic and this is part of our effort to keep it real," says Smith. "We have a subset of our vendors rank themselves on a scorecard each year, and then we rank them and provide recommendations for improvement, if appropriate. Then we review the gaps. It gives each vendor a taste of reality through our eyes. We replace the vendors that don't rank well or fail to improve. The two top performers get recognized with an award as our top vendors of choice."

Greg Smith's Vendor Scorecard

Please rank your company performance with WWF over the last year from 1–5 on the following characteristics, with 1 = low and 5 = high.

	1	2	3	4	5
1. Responsiveness/availability	☐	☐	☐	☐	☐
2. Quality of deliverables/work	☐	☐	☐	☐	☐
3. Customer service oriented	☐	☐	☐	☐	☐
4. Accuracy of work	☐	☐	☐	☐	☐
5. Value for WWF investment	☐	☐	☐	☐	☐
6. Communicates professionally (openly, consistently, effectively)	☐	☐	☐	☐	☐
7. Innovative work approaches	☐	☐	☐	☐	☐
8. Proactive recommendations to solve challenges	☐	☐	☐	☐	☐
9. Understands WWF business needs	☐	☐	☐	☐	☐
10. Quality of working relationships with key WWF staff	☐	☐	☐	☐	☐

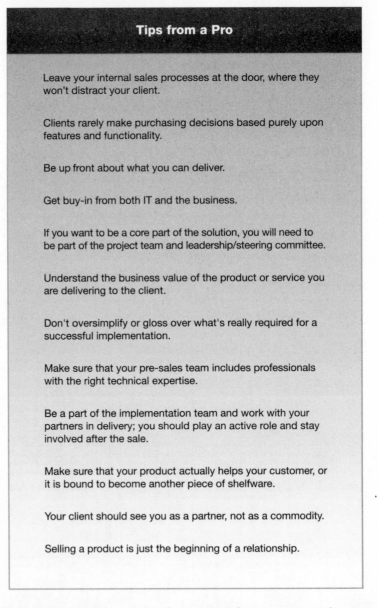

Tips from a Pro

Leave your internal sales processes at the door, where they won't distract your client.

Clients rarely make purchasing decisions based purely upon features and functionality.

Be up front about what you can deliver.

Get buy-in from both IT and the business.

If you want to be a core part of the solution, you will need to be part of the project team and leadership/steering committee.

Understand the business value of the product or service you are delivering to the client.

Don't oversimplify or gloss over what's really required for a successful implementation.

Make sure that your pre-sales team includes professionals with the right technical expertise.

Be a part of the implementation team and work with your partners in delivery; you should play an active role and stay involved after the sale.

Make sure that your product actually helps your customer, or it is bound to become another piece of shelfware.

Your client should see you as a partner, not as a commodity.

Selling a product is just the beginning of a relationship.

Figure 3.2   Valuable advice for vendors from a respected expert on IT delivery.
Source: Gary Fink, Accenture Partner.

And now we'd like to offer a suggestion: Vendors should develop their own performance scorecards and ask their clients to fill them out periodically during the sales and delivery phases of every project. At the top of every scorecard, in big letters, print these words: *"How'm I doin'?"*

Chapter FOUR

If You Aren't a Partner, Then You're a Commodity

"Examples of bad vendor behaviors: Rotating sales reps, sending inexperienced staff to handle complex issues and then expecting the CIO's organization to educate them."

Thornton May

Executive Director and Dean,
IT Leadership Academy

Here's a Real Cream Puff That Was Driven Only on Sundays

Before the Internet enabled consumers to compare prices at the click of a mouse, buying a car was an unnerving experience. The salesman made you feel ignorant, confused, and helpless. The color you wanted was never in stock. The option packages rarely made sense. Aftermarket products such as extended warranties, undercoating, and antitheft devices left your head spinning.

You left the showroom relieved to have purchased a car—and wondering just how much you'd been ripped off. It was an experience that you wouldn't wish on your worst enemy.

Then why do so many IT sales reps start acting like old-fashioned car salesmen whenever they get near a CIO? Surely it can't be in their DNA. To be fair, most automobile dealerships over the past couple of years have drastically changed their sales tactics, making them much more consumer friendly.

Faced with a new generation of Internet-empowered consumers and stiffer government regulations, automotive retailers shifted gears quickly. They developed new sales processes that are more in sync with the times and more customer friendly. It's an admirable example of an industry transforming itself on the fly.

It's time for the IT industry to start making similar changes. The days when an IT sales rep could treat a CIO like a high school kid looking to buy his first car are long gone. That CIO has grown up.

Leave Your Sales Process at the Door

As a salesperson, you've undoubtedly read dozens of books about sales strategies and have sat through hours of training sessions designed to improve your selling skills. Many sales books are genuinely interesting, and you almost always pick up some nugget of useful advice from a training seminar. But don't try to drag your CIO prospects through the latest, greatest sales process.

CIOs really don't care about your sales processes. And they especially don't like cheesy sales babble sprinkled throughout a presentation. If you find yourself using clichés such as, "What keeps you up at night?," then it's time to edit your sales pitch. Remember why you were invited to the CIO's office. Keep the conversation focused on solving problems and delivering value.

Too often, IT vendors focus more on their products and sales processes than on the client. That's a guaranteed turnoff, says Gary Fink of Accenture.

CIOs prefer working with IT suppliers who "recognize that selling the product is not the end of the process, but the beginning of a relationship," says Fink. IT suppliers with overbearing, anxiety-driven sales processes risk irritating and alienating their clients. Worse yet, they reduce their chances of success.

"The used car salesman approach is an annoyance that few clients appreciate and adds zero value," Fink says. "Being aggressive and persistent is critical to successful sales, but being *too* aggressive can actually make it harder for the client to concentrate on the real challenge at hand, which is finding the best solution to their business problem."

On the other hand, IT suppliers who are up front about what they can—and cannot—deliver are likely to have fewer serious issues with clients down the road. "Forthright honesty and authenticity are critical qualities for IT salespeople," says Fink. If the product has issues or limitations, explain them to the client early and offer both solutions and product plans for the future to address them. Inevitably, weaknesses will surface. But an honest discussion at the beginning of the sales process will reduce the likelihood of unpleasant surprises during the implementation.

"Showing the real shortfalls and blemishes of a product is a risk, but it's a practice that will build trust and understanding of how the product really fits. So it is really critical to provide an understanding of what those weaknesses are and how they can be addressed. Everyone needs to understand what the product does and doesn't do," says Fink.

It's also important for the vendor to carefully define the roles played by various members of the sales team. This avoids confusion and improves trust. For example, many vendors will pair a sales rep with a systems engineer or a technical architect. "This kind of arrangement works best when the roles are well delineated and separated," Fink says.

It's also important for the account team to keep these technical representatives involved throughout the sales process. Don't just bring them in to run demos. The client needs to know that the technical representatives are an integral part of the account team and that they will be available when they're needed. A best practice is sticking with the same technical reps throughout the sale. Some vendors designate a lead sales engineer or technical architect to stay with the customer throughout the project.

Act like a Consultant

In their visionary book *Clients for Life* Jagdish Sheth and Andrew Sobel explore the essential qualities of long-term business relationships. Early in the book, they offer this valuable observation:

If you sell a complex product or service that is critical to your client's business . . . your client will have a significant need for advice and consultation, and the opportunity exists for you to become an advisor to him rather than just a salesperson.

The book's final chapter, entitled "The Soul of the Great Professional," makes the argument for developing an "abundance mentality" that is constantly seeking new opportunities and is always generating fresh ideas.

Sheth and Sobel conclude that great professionals are mission oriented; they channel adversity into wisdom and confidence; they always view old clients as new clients; and they engage in continual self-renewal.

Their book contains almost no tactical advice—because great professionals:

- Are by nature strategic thinkers.

- Don't focus on selling; they focus on partnering.

- Look for opportunities to generate tangible business benefits for their clients over time.

- Tend to hang onto their clients longer and earn more income precisely because they're not perceived as selling products or services. Instead they're seen as helping clients grow their businesses.

- Are perceived the same way by their clients. They are seen as trusted advisors committed to providing value over the long haul.

How do you want your clients to see you? As a seller of products and services or as a trusted advisor who helps them expand their business?

Acting like a consultant requires "the ability to understand clients, understand what they need, and apply the appropriate domain expertise or capability to find the best solutions for them," says Accenture's Gary Fink.

"When the client thinks, 'He's trying to sell me something,' then you're still just selling," adds Fink. "When the client thinks, 'He's really trying to help me,' then you're acting like a consultant and that's when the relationship really begins."

Don't Play Pricing Games

Certainly one of the strangest quirks of the IT industry is the frantic wheeling and dealing that takes place at the end of every quarter and fiscal year.

"CIOs and purchasing departments are well aware of this and take full advantage of the opportunities to drive hard bargains," says David Read, the CEO of Prestige Purchasing, a U.K.-based consultancy. But such predictable antics can have negative results, making software vendors look like tactical players instead of strategic partners.

In their mad scramble to meet sales quotas, IT vendors convey the wrong message to their customers. "It seems as though they're more interested in one-night stands than marriages," says Read.

Widespread belief in Moore's Law makes it hard for IT vendors to argue convincingly that prices are on an upward trend. "Everyone believes that technology prices go down over time and that by waiting long enough the prices will go down even more," says Brad Miller, president of Perimeter Internetworking, an Internet security services provider based in Connecticut.

Price-based sales strategies aren't merely obsolete—they can be downright dangerous to the long-term financial health of an IT supplier. "The more you focus on the dollars, the more your customers will perceive your product as a commodity," adds Miller. "People can smell desperation. They'll assume that your company is in financial trouble or that no one else wants your product. Don't send that kind of signal."

Joe Choti, the CTO at Major League Baseball Advanced Media, finds it "preposterous" when IT sales reps try to run pricing games on him. "They'll tell me, 'I'm offering you this price and if you close the deal today, the price is what I quoted. But if you close tomorrow, I'm jacking up the price 20 percent.' Do they really expect me to believe that?"

CIOs are also irritated when IT suppliers try to confuse them by offering overly complicated licensing arrangements, or by changing the rules midway through a multiyear contract. "Licensing gets very tricky. It's crucial when you're negotiating a contract to understand exactly how the vendor is counting users," says Mary Finlay, deputy CIO of Partners Healthcare. "Sometimes vendors change their counting methodology. That can really sour a relationship."

Jeri Dunn, the former CIO of Tyson Foods, agrees:

When it comes to licensing, you've got to get everything spelled out in black and white because you don't want to get into an argument down the road. The worst thing that can happen is that you misinterpret or misunderstand the terms.

Nowadays the term "user" can mean anything. But there are many levels of users. There are casual users, named users, regular users and super users. Make sure you understand how the vendor defines "user" so there are no surprises.

Arguments over license fees can be especially vexing for CIOs of large, global companies with multiple sites. Several CIOs complained to us about vendors who charged the same license fee for all users, making no allowances for the differences between light users and heavy users.

"If you have 120,000 employees, you shouldn't have to pay the same fee for an employee using a self-service HR application and an employee making entries into a general ledger," says Dunn.

Sacrifice in Vain?

Ron Rose, the CIO of Priceline.com, wonders how much revenue and margin could be increased by anticipating the end of the quarter more effectively and closing the most critical sales earlier. "IT vendors give up a hefty amount of revenue and margin at the tail end of each quarter," observes Rose. "It would be interesting to know how much more they would earn if they could avoid even half of that."

For veteran CIOs, many IT sales pitches create an eerie sense of déjà vu. If the CIO shows little interest in the product, the sales rep quickly changes the subject to pricing. When that gambit fails, the sales rep assumes the CIO is merely being coy. At this point, the sales rep might begin talking about potential discounts or other incentives.

What the sales rep probably doesn't know—or refuses to believe—is that the CIO's budget was set months ago. Unless the supplier is riding to the rescue with an urgently needed product or service that will help the company address a pressing business challenge, there won't be any money in CIO's budget to cover the purchase.

Offering steeper discounts won't move the sale forward for two good reasons. The first is very simple: If zero dollars have been set aside for the purchase, a discount is meaningless. The second reason is that most CIOs have been around the block often enough to know instinctively that the first-year cost of any new IT purchase usually represents the tip of a much larger iceberg.

"If you're looking at an IT purchase from a business perspective, you're not just thinking about the initial costs. You're thinking about TCO (total cost of ownership), which includes continuing costs such as maintenance, upgrades and retraining," says Paul Zazzera.

So raising the promise of steep discounts on first-year costs moves the conversation in the wrong direction by immediately raising suspicions about the sales rep's motives. Since every CIO understands that sales reps have quotas, the CIOs can't help but wonder: How low will the price go?

"Then it turns into a game. The CIO tries to get the best possible discount. The supplier tries to hang onto his profit. The CIO knows that if he waits until 11:59 P.M. on December 31, he'll get the best price," says Zazzera. "It's really a vicious cycle. I can't think of another industry in which there are so many cliffhanger deals."

Almost all of the CIOs we interviewed for this book describe the rush to close deals at the end of a quarter or the end of a year as an ugly, industrywide epidemic. Mary Finlay recalls the time a vendor rep showed up at her office on Christmas Eve. "She was begging me to sign the agreement, saying it was the end of the quarter and that she wouldn't make her numbers unless I signed. But that's not how we do business. I said, 'Merry Christmas and I'll talk with you in January.'"

Another sales rep left Finlay a message saying that if he didn't finalize a pending deal over the weekend, the price would go up. "I didn't even call him back—but I called his VP on Monday," she recalls.

Ray Hill, the chief procurement officer at Pitney-Bowes, remembers when two reps from an ERP vendor spent part of their Christmas vacations at his home trying to finalize a deal. "I knew we would get a better price because they were so desperate to close the deal before the end of the year," says Hill.

In many cases, however, there will be no deal—no matter how low the price goes. "Very few people are going to start sharpening their pencils at the last minute to figure out if a deal is worth doing," says Zazzera. "We don't want to have to buy like that. But that said, many companies don't offer their best deals until the last minute."

Put Skin in the Game

Like any other cutting edge science, information technology is full of unknowns. Every IT project is accompanied by a degree of risk and uncertainty. Because no two implementations are exactly alike, every IT project is an experiment. That's just the nature of the beast.

In the early days of IT, suppliers expected their customers to accept the uncertainty and assume a large burden of the risk. Faced with few choices, most customers were forced to acquiesce.

The modern CIO won't roll over so easily. Today the CIO wants you, the IT supplier, to minimize the uncertainty and to share the risk. The CIO expects you to put skin in the game.

One of the best ways for an IT supplier to put skin in the game is by conducting a proof of concept (POC) trial, says Brian Margolies, vice president of IT planning and international operations at Scholastic, the world's largest publisher and distributor of children's books.

Many vendors worry about the costs of conducting a POC. Some vendors see requests for POCs as attempts by their clients to get something for free without making a sincere commitment.

Those concerns are ungrounded. The cost of a POC is almost always recoverable. And the notion that a client would request a POC simply to "kick the tires" assumes that the client has nothing better to do with their time and resources than conduct tests of a vendor's product.

"We don't have the resources to pilot unproven technologies," says Margolies, "so we find it very helpful when a vendor is willing to put skin in the game during the presales phase by working with us on a proof of concept. A POC lets us see the implications of a purchase from a standpoint of cost, performance, and functionality. It gives us a reasonable idea of what we're getting into."

A POC also enables Margolies to access whether the supplier's technology will operate properly in Scholastic's environment. From his perspective, a POC creates the potential for a win-win scenario by reducing Scholastic's risk while giving the supplier an opportunity to earn the company's trust.

"A POC generally irons out the kinks, which makes it easier when it comes to contracting because we know what to expect," says Margolies. "A POC can be a great way of showing that you value us as a customer, because it proves that you're willing to make an investment up front to earn our business. It makes us feel more comfortable about bringing our resources to the table."

POCs can also deepen relationships with customers, making it easier to sell across several business units of the same enterprise. "Never assume that everyone talks to each other about day-to-day issues, especially across divisions," advises Margolies. "In one particular instance, a POC helped us bring together two of our organizations so they could collaborate on a joint project. That was a big accomplishment."

In this case, the supplier's willingness to arrange a POC created opportunities for two organizations within Scholastic to see how one solution might resolve the needs of both. "We had two different groups with converging needs. Each group was budgeted to do a separate project. The POC actually helped these two entities understand that their issues were very similar, which enabled us to leverage a single investment to address both of their needs," says Margolies.

The POC led to a win-win situation for the supplier and for Scholastic. More important, it created a bond of trust. The supplier earned its seat in the CIO's inner circle by proving its willingness to put skin in the game.

Other ways to put skin in the game include providing expertise at your own expense during the pre-sales cycle and helping the CIO figure out strategies for leveraging the value of existing technology investments. Offering pre-sales, value-added consulting demonstrates a vendor's commitment, expertise, and empathy.

Yes, the process of putting skin in the game will cost you money, time, and effort. Consider it an investment. Or think of it as table stakes. Either way, you've got to put skin in the game if you want to play.

Be Candid about Your Ability to Deliver Global Deals

About five years ago, many large companies began moving aggressively toward global contracting with key IT suppliers. The general belief was that it would be easier to deal with a smaller number of large vendors than with dozens or even hundreds of smaller vendors.

As a best practice, vendor consolidation seemed to make sense for a variety of reasons: It would save money, streamline the process of managing contracts, and make it easier to standardize technology platforms.

However, there were unexpected side effects. In many instances, vendors couldn't deliver the truly global deals that their clients expected. Instead of actually reducing complexity, some companies discovered that they had merely shifted the responsibility for dealing with complexity to the vendors.

Almost every CIO whom we interviewed complained to us about the difficulties and hassles of global deals. In some cases, according to the CIOs, IT account teams offered global deals without making absolutely certain that their organizations had the resources in place to fulfill a global contract.

Bob Turner, a partner at Software Licensing Consultants, Inc., specializes in contract negotiation and licensing issues. He urges IT vendors to be upfront and completely honest about their capabilities for delivering global deals.

"Make sure your account team isn't promising a global deal if they can't deliver it," says Turner. "These deals are difficult. There will be areas that simply aren't under your control. Be candid with the CIO about which parts of the deal you control, and which parts you don't. For example, if you're on the account team, you probably can't control the legal part of the deal. But you can control your comp plan. Explain that to the CIO so he understands exactly what to expect from you."

Turner says there are five areas in which IT vendors typically struggle with global contracting:

1. *Structure.* Some vendors have global subsidiaries and affiliates that are prevented by contract from licensing

software, selling hardware, or performing professional services in each other's designated territory. Each territory typically has its own licensing and pricing structure. The structures might not be consistent from territory to territory, which makes it very difficult to reach a global agreement.

2. *Compensation and quotas.* Some vendors are structured so that each country has its own P&L (profit and loss) responsibility. The country managers have a revenue quota and they are very reluctant to relinquish control of a sales opportunity within their country, even if it jeopardizes a much larger deal.

3. *Philosophical differences.* Licensing and pricing philosophies differ from country to country. Some cultures take pride in their negotiating skills and don't believe in discounting heavily to win business. They believe that discounting "de-values" the software. Other cultures have adopted the "win at all costs" approach to business and won't hesitate to offer steep discounts if it will help them close a deal. Cultural differences from country to country or region to region can make negotiating global agreements difficult, especially when you are trying to get approvals from all the interested parties.

4. *Legal obstacles.* The laws for licensing software vary from country to country. Drafting a global license agreement that meets the requirements of all jurisdictions is not a simple matter. Some vendors choose not to license globally because they know how difficult it

can be to meet the legal requirements of multiple jurisdictions.

5. *Emotional issues.* Global deals can provoke a range of highly emotional reactions since they affect compensation and generally take control away from country managers and local sales teams. Global agreements can lead to internecine squabbling in which sales executives refuse to relinquish control of their deals. Global deals can ignite wide-ranging internal disputes that most IT vendors are unprepared to cope with.

What's the best way of handling all these potential problems? Again, the best strategy is forthright honesty. When a CIO starts talking about a global contract, be prepared to discuss your abilities and limitations with complete candor. Address the issues you can control and be clear about the areas in which your influence is limited.

Sometimes your best source of information about global deals will be the client. If the client has negotiated global contracts in the past, ask for his or her advice. Ask the client to show you examples of successful global deals. Ask how they solved global challenges with previous vendors. Then you can begin assembling your own list of best practices for global contracting.

It's a sure bet that more of your clients will be seeking global contracts, and they'll be looking to you for guidance and expertise. The more prepared you are to deal candidly with all the various issues of global contracting, the less likely it is that you'll be tempted to make promises you cannot keep.

Bring a Vision

CIOs don't expect IT vendors to act like philosopher kings. But they do appreciate it when IT vendors offer fresh ideas for solving difficult IT challenges.

"A good IT salesperson should be able to think in a visionary way," says Harvey Koeppel, former CIO of the Global Consumer Group at Citigroup, the world's preeminent financial services company. "At the same time, a good IT salesperson should know how to think tactically, understand a concept, and break it down into manageable pieces."

The ideal IT salesperson, says Koeppel, is a "pragmatic visionary" who possesses high-level reasoning skills and specific, hands-on knowledge of relevant IT processes.

"I don't expect a salesperson to come into my office and say, 'This is my vision for 2010.' I do, however, expect to have an intelligent dialogue," says Koeppel.

The ideal salesperson should be capable of mapping technology products and services quickly and transparently to specific business issues, says Koeppel. "I want to know that you have a similar value system, that you know the industry, that you've walked a mile in my shoes, and that you

understand the challenges and opportunities facing my organization," he says.

Koeppel advises salespeople to keep the client's environment in mind while painting a picture of the future. "I
might think that you're bringing me a really cool idea. But
at the same time, I'm wondering if what you're talking
about will be viable at our organization. It might be a
great concept, but will it run on our infrastructure? Will it
be compatible with our standards? Will it ever see the light
of day?"

When a client raises such questions, the salesperson's
practical knowledge of technology is really put to the test.
When meeting with forward-thinking CIOs like Koeppel,
you can't rely on small talk about sports to keep the conversation going. Be prepared to engage the CIO in a dialogue
about the concerns weighing most heavily on his mind,
such as:

- How outsourcing must be an organic extension of
  the IT supplier's brand, not just a "point in time"
  transaction.

- Why complex solution stacks are considered yesterday's IT and why simplicity is seen as the future of IT.

- The crucial differences between BPO (business process
  outsourcing) and KPO (knowledge process outsourcing) strategies.

- Privacy, compliance, and information security.

- Wireless technology.

- The impact of Web 2.0 on consumerism.

- How collaboration is transforming IT.

Your clients are unlikely to fault you for sounding too intelligent. But they'll also want proof that you know what you're talking about.

Crank Up Your Empathy

Thornton May is one of our favorite IT thought leaders. If you're not familiar with his work, you're missing out on some genuinely useful intelligence about the current state of IT management. May is an executive education faculty member at the Anderson Graduate School of Management at U.C.L.A.; the Haas School of Business at U.C.-Berkeley; and Carnegie-Mellon University. He also serves on the Curriculum Advisory Committee at Babson College.

His work has appeared in the *Harvard Business Review*, the *Wall Street Journal*, the *M.I.T. Sloan Management Review*, *American Demographics*, *U.S.A. Today*, and *Business-Week*. He's even testified before Congress, speaking as an expert witness on large technology implementations.

We mention all of this because it's important for you to know that when he talks, CIOs listen. May and his research team produce *CIO Habitat*, a monthly report on trends and patterns in IT strategy. A recent issue focused on IT vendor management, and its findings support our central contention that CIOs aren't looking for the best price when they go shopping for IT. They're looking for the best partners.

May wrote about a CIO who described his inner circle of trusted suppliers as "soul mates on a journey to the same destination." He also quotes an exchange between a CIO and a CEO, in which the CEO rebukes the CIO for referring to IT suppliers as vendors. The CEO tells the CIO that vendors "fill candy machines." Suppliers, on the other hand, "are trusted partners, critical to the success of the enterprise and are to be treated with respect."

The CEO's enlightened attitude shows that he understands how crucial it is for the CIO to form trusting relationships with his IT suppliers. The CEO grasps that the success of the IT organization depends on the CIO's ability to choose the right IT suppliers and maintain long-term, stable relationships with them.

We should stop right here to acknowledge that not every CEO is so enlightened and that not every CIO is fully conscious of his or her absolutely crucial need to identify a select group of trusted suppliers.

Consciously or unconsciously, however, the CIO needs your empathy. If you're wondering exactly what empathy means in this context, it's helpful to remember that it's derived from a Greek word meaning "to suffer with."

If you can feel the CIO's pain, you've got empathy. If you can imagine yourself walking in the CIO's shoes, you've got empathy. When May and his team talk about empathy, what they really mean is your ability to understand in a very profound sense what the CIO is responsible for achieving.

Empathizing with the CIO also requires you to resist bad behaviors that jeopardize long-term relationships. May lists three specific ways in which IT suppliers ruin perfectly good relationships with CIOs:

Bad Vendor Behaviors	Examples
Attitude problems	Presenting solutions without taking the time to make sure they make sense for the CIO's organization, aggressively selling unwanted services, setting unrealistic expectations and not taking responsibility for problems.
Process failures	Slow response to questions or problems, communication drop-offs after contract is signed, pricing strategies that don't align with the customer's internal processes.
People mistakes	Rotating sales reps, sending inexperienced staff to handle complex issues and then expecting the CIO's organization to educate them.

Different CIOs will have different goals and agendas. It won't be easy to map the individual agendas of all the CIOs in your territory. But if you want to be truly effective in this industry, you'll need to know your customers better than they know themselves. Then you can support, coach, and guide them down the path to success.

Chapter FIVE

Communication Is Crucial

"I was just astounded at the cavalier way in which some vendors dealt with critical issues such as privacy and confidentiality. Sometimes it amazed me."

Jeri Dunn
Former CIO, Tyson Foods

Stop Gabbing and Start Communicating

The ability to communicate requires more than a gift for gab. As one CIO artfully put it, "Sales reps will talk to anyone, about anything. They'll even talk to rocks."

Communicating is another matter entirely. Bill Babcock, chairman of Babcock & Jenkins, a marketing agency in Oregon with IT-industry clients including Microsoft, Adobe, Symantec, and Siemens, says communicating successfully with a busy CIO requires self-discipline, focus, and planning.

CIOs, Babcock says, are "easy to target, tricky to reach and hard to hold." In an excellent white paper titled "Marketing to the CIO, Technical Decision Makers, and Technical Influencers," Babcock writes about a hypothetical CIO named George who has difficulty delegating, but knows that he needs outside expertise to help him make good business decisions.

The keys to getting through to him are sliding past the gatekeeper with something she doesn't dare toss, grabbing his attention, and then keeping every communication as relevant and brief as possible. He doesn't want to be sold, he wants to be smart. He won't talk to a salesperson until he's on a level playing field. Give him condensed nuggets of highly relevant expertise and he'll stay engaged. Get ahead of the selling cycle and the doors close.

"Immediate ROI" are the magic words for gaining entry to this CIO's inner circle. Any supplier who shows "an immediate ROI for a new technology will get consideration," Babcock writes. The CIO "needs to see short payback for any investment."

But vendors must offer more than talk. They must communicate in language the CIO understands and appreciates. "It's just not enough any more to talk about increased profitability through increased productivity or efficiency. He's seen peers get fired for swallowing that line. If a vendor talks upping the ROI, she or he better have rock-solid proof," writes Babcock.

Be prepared to offer relevant examples to support your assertions. Case studies retelling the experiences of other companies are often the most effective tools for driving home your messages. "Good ROI storytelling is the secret ingredient of highly compelling and effective business cases," according to Jack M. Keen and Bonnie Digrius, authors of *Making Technology Investments Profitable*.

"Clever storytelling is one of the quickest and most effective ways to gain executive understanding, buy-in and funding. It also helps attract support and cooperation from reluctant users during project implementation and operation," writes Keen, the founder and president of The Deciding Factor, a global provider of ROI business case tools and consulting.

When building a business case, he says, "vivid stories translate dry, abstract numbers into compelling pictures" with emotional as well as intellectual appeal.

Keen and Digrius observe that many sales reps spend "too much time on numbers and too little time explaining their significance."

In many instances, the best way to communicate with a CIO is to introduce her to another CIO who has had a similar experience. Make the introductions informally. Sponsor a seminar or an executive lunch. As you well know, many large IT suppliers stage regular events to highlight their latest products. These events invariably feature presentations from thought leaders, gurus, and industry celebrities.

Despite their predictable nature, many of the events offer excellent opportunities for you to network your customers with each other and with your prospects. Whether you call it "reverse marketing," "community marketing," or "peer-to-peer marketing," it's an extremely effective tactic.

Almost every CIO and technology executive whom we interviewed told us that they tend not to believe anything they hear from a sales rep until it's validated by a peer. That's an awfully powerful statement. Your ads might look nice and maybe your booth at the trade show is truly spectacular. But at the end of the day, the kind of marketing that works in this industry travels by word of mouth. Look at Figures 5.1 and 5.2.

Effective Vendor Communication Methods (a)

Peer recommendations

In-person meetings

Articles in technology publications

Vendor web site

Executive conferences or events

Trade shows

Webcasts

Personal e-mail communication

Vendor-sponsored supplements

0%   10   20   30   40   50   60   70   80   90   100%

■ Effective   ■ Neutral   ■ Not effective

Figure 5.1   CIOs respond differently to different forms of communication. Are your marketing dollars spent wisely?
Source: Adapted from *CIO* magazine research project, "The Role and Influence of the 21st Century CIO."

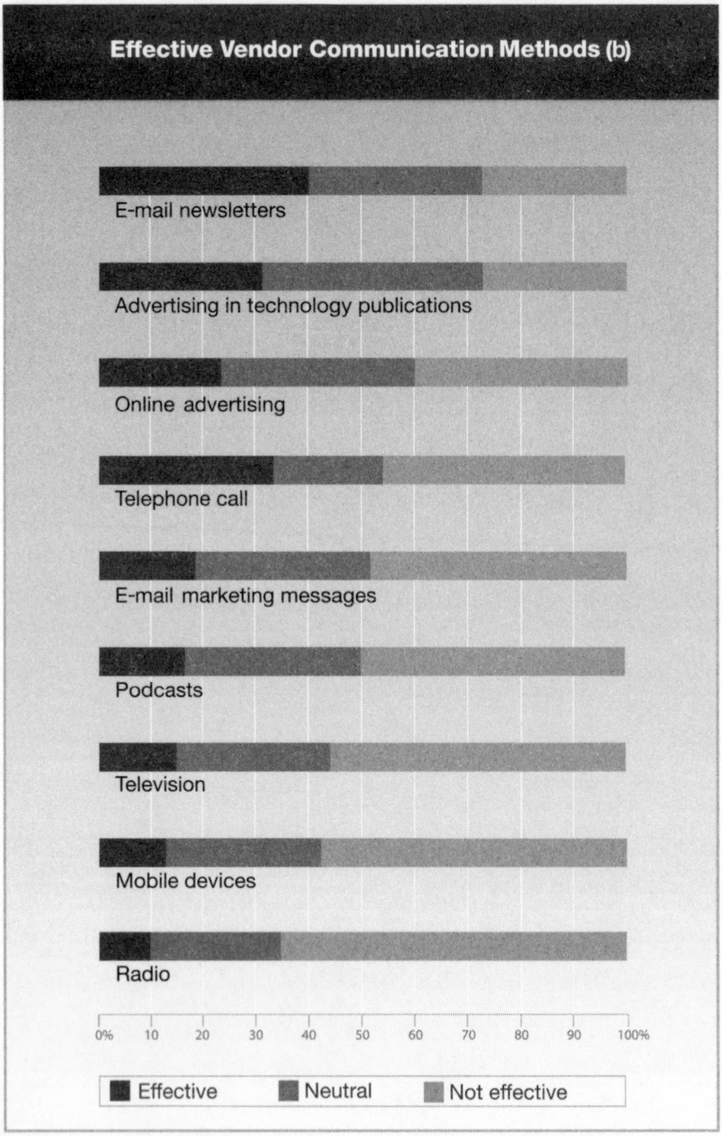

Effective Vendor Communication Methods (b)

- E-mail newsletters
- Advertising in technology publications
- Online advertising
- Telephone call
- E-mail marketing messages
- Podcasts
- Television
- Mobile devices
- Radio

0% 10 20 30 40 50 60 70 80 90 100%

■ Effective   ■ Neutral   ■ Not effective

Figure 5.2 Choosing the optimum channel for your marketing messages isn't easy. Are you making the right choices?
Source: Adapted from *CIO* magazine research project, "The Role and Influence of the 21st Century CIO."

Don't Rely on "Push" Marketing Only

David Munn is president and CEO of the IT Services Marketing Association (ITSMA). Based in Lexington, Massachusetts, ITSMA is a membership community for executives who market and sell technology-related services and solutions. A recent ITSMA survey, "How Customers Choose Solution Providers," shows clearly that when executives consider technology purchases, their first step is to seek advice from professional peers.

"CIOs talk to each other. The experiences they have with your organization become fodder for the stories they share with their peers," says Munn. "If you're a vendor, you need to ensure that you're delivering more than just technology. Are you helping solve a particular business problem? Are you meeting budget and time commitments? Are you flexible and responsive? Are you transferring knowledge? These are the types of things marketers today need to think about in order to create real customer advocates for their brands. Marketing can no longer be just concerned with traditional marketing activities."

The survey also confirms what the CIOs we interviewed told us: Unsolicited e-mails and cold calls are mostly ineffective. According to the survey data, customers read only 17 percent of unsolicited e-mails they receive and respond to only 13 percent of the cold calls they receive.

"So many inbound or 'push' marketing activities are too vague, untargeted, impersonal, and ultimately irrelevant," says

Munn. "CIOs just tune them out. They're under intense pressure from their organizations to grow the business. They don't have time to return 99 percent of the cold calls they get."

The survey also shows that 66 percent of the time, customers proactively look for information about technology they're interested in acquiring. Only 34 percent of the time do they wait for vendors to contact them first.

Influencing the Influencers

Munn recommends five levers that will help vendors market their offerings more successfully and win more deals:

1. Build an army of advocates by making sure your customers have good experiences with the products and services you market, sell, and deliver.

2. Invest in relationship-building activities such as peer networking events, user group meetings, advisory boards, and councils where no sales talk is allowed. Activities such as these will make you a more valuable resource to your customers, positioning you as an advisor instead of yet another marketer jockeying for attention.

3. Influence the influencers. In the past, you could create buzz for a product or service by calling a handful of trade journalists and industry analysts. Today, the CIO responds to a much larger circle of influencers that includes peers, consultants, integrators, outsourcers, partners, advisors, and even bloggers. Make sure that your marketing also targets these influencers.

4. Balance "push" and "pull" marketing. The ITSMA survey shows that only one-third of the executives who have a need for a technology solution are contacted first by a vendor with their push marketing tactics such as direct sales, telemarketing, direct mail, or e-mail. The other two-thirds of those executives go out and proactively look for solution providers themselves by either speaking to peers or researching available options. That's where pull marketing tactics such as search engine optimization, industry seminars, case studies, published articles, and conference presentations prove their value. Unfortunately, most vendors don't invest enough in pull marketing to take advantage of the opportunities created by customers who would prefer to find their own information instead of relying on marketers to provide it.

5. Use Account-Based Marketing (a term coined by ITSMA) to target niche audiences more efficiently. Account-Based Marketing treats individual companies as "markets of one," making it far easier to deliver effective marketing messages to key influencers and decision makers. Think of Account-Based Marketing as one-to-one marketing for the business-to-business world.

"We also learned from our survey that technology executives will pay attention to marketing messages that convey useful information," says Munn.

For example, 75 percent of respondents replied "yes" when the ITSMA survey asked, "Would you read unsolicited marketing materials that contain ideas that might be relevant to your business such as success stories, research reports, and Webinar invitations?" and 92 percent of those respondents said "yes" when the survey asked, "Would you pay attention to these marketing materials even if they were from solution providers you had not previously done business with?"

These are important findings that demonstrate which kind of marketing materials are most likely to generate responses from CIOs and other technology executives.

Remove Complexity from Your Organization

In the late 1990s, when IT suppliers made the leap from selling tools to providing solutions, their organizations became radically more complex. IT suppliers raced for competitive advantages by building larger solution stacks with more features and greater functionality, making it nearly impossible for a single pre-sales resource to cover an entire solution suite.

Recognizing this dilemma, IT suppliers added specialists to cover niche areas such as data warehousing, analytics, and security.

As the shift in emphasis from products to domain expertise continued, IT suppliers reorganized internally to serve the specific needs of vertical markets such as financial services, media, entertainment, telecom, manufacturing, energy, life sciences, healthcare, transportation, consumer package goods, retail, and automotive.

Out of this specialization emerged new positions such as Supply Chain Strategist, Manufacturing, Risk Specialist, Financial Services, and CRM Program Manager, Telecommunications. Some of the titles we've all seen recently on business cards really make us wonder how far the trend toward specialization will go. See Figure 5.3.

From the perspective of the IT suppliers, creating larger, deeper, and broader organizations to serve the different

Figure 5.3   Confusing Business Card

needs of different customer groups makes perfect sense. But from the CIO's perspective, it can be a nightmare.

Yes, CIOs *do* appreciate the efforts made by IT suppliers to broaden the range of their products and services. At the same time, CIOs *do not* want to spend an eternity navigating through a supplier's multilayered organization.

CIOs repeatedly told us how much they value suppliers who make it easy for them to find the information and resources they need within the supplier's organization. They also told us about how often they were disappointed by sales reps who were unfamiliar with their own organizations, had insufficient clout to influence other parts of their organizations, or were just plain unwilling to use their clout to help their customers.

CIOs need help finding their way around your organization. Make sure there is a solid connection and smooth transition from the pre-sales stage to the post-sales stage of every project. Don't turn account transition or rep turnover into your customer's problem.

Your organization has a wealth of resources, but many of them are hidden, hard to find, or difficult to utilize. If you don't have the bandwidth to serve as a guide, try to line up an executive sponsor for the account, who can escalate critical issues and even provide continuity when account reps are changed out. See Figure 5.4.

Figure 5.4   Coordinating Your Organization and the CIO's

Seeking Multiple Relationships

When vendors are supplying business-critical products or services, David King, the CIO at Regal Entertainment Group, establishes relationships at multiple levels within the vendor's organization. "I want our day-to-day operations people to have relationships with the vendor's day-to-day operations people, and I want our VPs to have relationships with the vendor's VPs. As the CIO, I need to have relationships with the vendor's CEO and top executives."

Even a vendor with a transaction-driven sales force can become a good strategic partner—as long as there are designated relationship managers within the vendor's organization.

Still, King says he would have "second thoughts" about a supplier of business-critical solutions who would not support a network of multiple relationships.

"There are two good reasons for creating multiple relationships between the customer and the vendor. Number one is that when an issue is identified, it can be escalated smoothly and resolved. Number two is that many large vendors are just not very nimble. It takes a lot of steady pressure from a lot of different people to nudge them in a new direction that might benefit both of our organizations. Multiple relationships make that process of gentle nudging more doable."

It's not ego-tripping when King attempts to exert a measure of influence over his vendors. It's good business practice. Sometimes a CIO can see the future more clearly than a vendor. When King subtly nudges a vendor, it's usually because the vendor doesn't understand the potential value of a new product or service. Gentle prodding from CIOs like King can help vendors recoup R&D investments, capture new streams of revenue, and identify new markets.

Be Accessible and Responsive

Resist the temptation to assume that your clients consider you accessible and responsive just because your company has a 24/7 tech support hotline.

Bear the responsibility for making sure that your customers are networked and connected properly across your organization. If your customer has a question about billing, it's your responsibility to make sure that someone in accounting responds helpfully. If your customer has an issue with one of your company's consultants, pick up the phone and call the consultant's manager. Don't make the customer do your work, unless you're willing to pay the price down the road.

Many organizations offer great support and ancillary services. But as we noted earlier, it can be difficult for customers to navigate their way through your organization, especially if you've recently merged with another supplier or have been acquired.

Merely having resources isn't enough. You have to make them available to the customer, which means you have got to be willing to serve as a guide and facilitator when the customer needs help.

Bruce C. Barnes, the president and CEO of Bold Vision, an IT management consultancy based in Ohio, recommends Radar O'Reilly as the perfect role model for sales reps and account managers. "Radar O'Reilly is always right there when you need him and sometimes he's there before you even realize that you need him," says Barnes, a former CIO himself. "Basically, you want to make it easy for your customers to do business with you," says Barnes. "Make it easy for them to find you and to communicate with you. If your customers can't get reach you when they need you, that's deadly." Sometimes you need to act like an old-fashioned social secretary, making introductions and even appointments for your customer to make certain that he or she meets the various people at your organization who will help them.

"Make sure that your customer also gets to know people outside of your department," he recommends. "The more connected your customer feels with your entire organization, the longer your relationship will last."

Respect Privacy

Since IT plays an absolutely crucial role at most organizations today, IT salespeople frequently participate in conversations involving the most highly sensitive aspects of a client's business. As an IT rep, you routinely see information that is regarded by the customer—and in some cases, by state or federal law—as secret, confidential, competitive, proprietary, or personal.

It's imperative that you regard your relationship with your prospects and customers as sacrosanct, and that you treat their information with the same care and respect that you would treat your own personal information.

Perhaps you just met with a telecom organization looking for help because their churn rate is out of control this quarter. Maybe you're pitching an Internet security solution to a regional bank, or selling financial management software to a large metropolitan hospital.

You're going to see and hear information that you cannot repeat. If this advice seems simplistic, read this anecdote from Jeri Dunn, formerly of Tyson Foods:

I had three people tell me that they'd overheard our IT consultants talking about Tyson in our local airport. The con-

sultants were just sitting there in the airport, having a con-
versation. But the people sitting behind them were Tyson em-
ployees. I called the senior partner of the consulting firm and
read him the riot act.

As they said in World War II, "loose lips sink ships." If
you think nobody's listening to your conversation, just remember those IT consultants at the airport. Blabbing away
about a client's confidential information—and getting caught
red-handed—is a sure way to be kicked out of the CIO's inner circle.

"I was just astounded at the cavalier way in which some
vendors dealt with critical issues such as privacy and confidentiality. Sometimes it amazes me," says Dunn.

Let the CIO Guide You to the Right Decision Maker

Suzanne Gordon, the CIO at SAS, tells an illuminating story
about an IT sales rep from a large help desk software firm
who kept pestering her with phone calls. "He called me about
a million times," Gordon recalls. "I kept telling him to speak
with our help desk manager and explain the product. If the
manager was interested in the product, we would pursue it."

Instead, the sales rep kept calling Gordon. Exasperated,
she asked him why he refused to stop calling her. He explained that his boss had given him a quota, and that he
was required to call a certain number of CIOs every month
to hit the quota.

Tips from a Pro

Be customer-focused, not speaker-focused.
It doesn't matter how much you know. What matters is how much you've learned and how much you care.

Be aware of "perception vs. reality."
How the CIO perceives you and your organization is reality. You and the other members of the account team might think a meeting went well, but what really counts is the client's perception. Before giving everyone on your team a high five, make sure the client was satisfied with the outcome of the meeting.

Engage your client.
Your job is engaging the CIO. Engagement means getting the CIO to listen, respond, and interact with you.

Keep industry jargon out of your presentations.
The CIO is bombarded with information from hundreds of vendors. CIOs hate hearing the same old gobbledygook. Do yourself a favor and stop using tired expressions such as, "Our solution is end-to-end, robust, and scalable." Your language should sound natural and relevant, not canned.

Have a conversation, don't present.
CIOs want an intelligent conversation, not a 30-slide presentation downloaded from your company's intranet. Here's the best way to structure a conversation:
- Define your position.
- Share a story that illustrates your position.
- Clearly state the moral, lesson, or point of the story.

Don't throw spaghetti on the wall.
Cover three to four key points in a conversation, not seven or eight. Each key point should have no more than three relevant subpoints. Each key point should be accompanied by a story illustrating the point.

Never "wing it."
Prepare for all meetings, even if you think you already know everything about the client. Follow a pre-meeting process and complete a client assessment. Ask yourself: What do they want to know, what do they need to know, what is their knowledge level on the topic? Remember the saying, "If you fail to plan, you plan to fail."

Figure 5.5 Excellent advice from a veteran consultant in the technology communications field.
Source: Bart Queen, C3 Communications.

Now what kind of sales tactic is that? Worse, the sales rep failed to realize that Gordon had helped him by guiding him directly to the individual with the most influence over purchasing decisions related to help desk products.

The moral here is that when the CIO says that she's too busy to speak with you and suggests that you call someone else within her organization, she isn't doing you a disservice—she's doing you a favor because now you know whom to speak with to move your sale forward.

Chapter SIX

IT Governance

"Part of IT governance is making sure that things get done. . . . There has to be a process. If there's no process, we never get where we're trying to go."

William J. Sweeney

Managing Director of Global Risk, Compliance, and Legal Technology, Corporate Investment Bank, Citigroup

Don't Assume That Everyone Plays by the Same Rules

Not long ago, we listened as Michael Lewis, author of *Moneyball*, spoke to an audience of IT executives about lessons the corporate world can learn from Major League Baseball. He touched on many fascinating topics and told intriguing stories. One that stuck in our minds was about how Billy Beane, the visionary general manager of the low-budget Oakland As, had established standard management processes across the organization's farm system.

Beane did this so players could be transferred from one team to another within the A's organization with as little sense of dislocation as possible. He knew instinctively that if he could ratchet down the level of confusion, the players would be more productive.

It would be nice to think that one day someone like Billy Beane will come along to standardize IT governance processes across all the companies in the world. As it stands today, it seems that every company practices IT governance in its unique manner.

That's the harsh reality facing IT suppliers. IT governance is a subset of corporate governance, which makes it something of an organizational orphan. Unlike finance, which has evolved standard procedures over centuries of practice, IT has little in the way of tradition or history to guide it. And because only a handful of CIOs have moved on to become CEOs, it's fair to say that IT governance issues are not particularly well understood at the topmost levels of many organizations.

"People all assume there's this federated style of governance and there's somehow this combination of business and IT people sitting together making joint decisions across a whole bunch of business units," says Ellen Kitzis of Gartner. "Unfortunately, that assumption is often wrong," she adds. "At many organizations, critical decisions affecting IT are made at the business unit level."

Still, there's an accelerating trend toward greater centralization of IT purchasing authority under the IT governance umbrella. At some corporations, IT works closely with corporate procurement and has significant influence over final purchasing decisions. That can create problems for sales reps who are accustomed to working directly with business units. Indeed, IT sales reps often waste time and energy presenting demos to executives with no purchasing power—simply because they haven't taken the trouble to familiarize themselves with a company's IT governance processes.

Keep Your Eye on the Steering Committee

Even when an organization doesn't have an elaborate IT governance process, key IT investment decisions are often determined by a steering committee made up of the CEO, the CFO, business unit executives, lawyers, and other interested parties. Says Kitzis:

> *Sales people really should think about the steering committee. The steering committee is looking at a couple of things. They're looking at things like the cost, in the business case, but more than anything, they're also looking at the portfolio. I think it's important for sales people to understand that. Sometimes they view their project as the only project that the company cares about. The reality is that at any one moment in time an average CIO probably has 25 or 30 significant projects underway.*

At some organizations, the CIO supervises a dozen or more project managers, each with eight or nine projects. "Think about it," notes Kitzis. "Your project sits somewhere in that portfolio of IT projects. The steering committee isn't going to overload that portfolio."

She advises IT sales reps to find out from the CIO where their project ranks relative to other projects on the CIO's plate. Even if the project you're pitching offers a great return and a competitive advantage, it might be one of several similar projects already underway. If that's the case, it's unlikely that the CIO's steering committee would add another project, even if it seems worthy and well-supported.

Here's our advice: Find out everything you can about the CIO's steering committee. The more you know about the steering committee and its priorities, the more you can help the CIO prepare for its questions.

Of course, there are situations in which IT governance is affected directly by external forces such as government regulation. The healthcare industry is a good example of this.

"The Health Insurance Portability and Accountability Act (HIPAA) requires us to pay special attention to privacy and confidentiality," explains Mary Finlay, deputy CIO of Boston-based Partners Healthcare. "We're highly regulated and we need to go through a very rigorous process to make sure that we're comfortable with all the safeguards vendors have in place. Most vendors with experience in our industry know this before they even approach us."

"We're Not Bending"

Meet William J. Sweeney, managing director of global risk, compliance, and legal technology for the corporate investment bank at Citigroup. He's responsible for the technology used by the bank to manage all of its market risk, credit risk, and operational risk.

He's also responsible for the technology that supports the bank's global compliance and legal operations, including case management, document management, electronic discovery, and e-mail supervision. In his spare time, he says

with grim humor, he also is responsible for co-managing the
bank's Basel compliance program.

With those kinds of responsibilities on his shoulders,
Sweeney can be excused for taking a hard line on IT governance. "I expect an IT vendor to be familiar with our
IT governance process," he says. "When a sales rep comes
in to meet me, the first thing I tell him is that he'd better
understand our governance process because we're not
bending."

Some IT sales reps try to go around Sweeney or avoid
him altogether. That's a short-sighted strategy, he says. "Always start with the person in charge of the technology
you're selling," he advises. "That person can help you get
into procurement, standards, engineering, information security—all those different parts of the organization that must
eventually participate in a purchasing decision. A smart vendor, says Sweeney, understands the value of building relationships with the IT managers who are ultimately
responsible for making sure that the technology the vendor
sells actually works. "They know all the internal processes
and they can walk you through them." Attempts to circum-
vent IT governance processes are usually counterproduc-
tive, he says.

When pressed, Sweeney concedes that IT governance
can appear confusing to an outsider. "We have standard
processes, but we don't have a single standard process. We
have a whole series of guidelines around critical processes

like development, information security, operational readiness, vendor selection, and vendor management."

Despite the complexities, the supplier is responsible for sorting through the details and following the procedures correctly. The more trusted you are by the CIO, the more likely he or she will be to help you through the maze.

Keeping It Real

For Sweeney, IT governance covers a wide territory. "There's the financial component of IT governance that says it's my job to ensure that for every dollar we spend, we get $1.10 worth of value. Another part of IT governance is making sure that the technologies people *think* they need are actually needed," he explains.

It's natural for IT sales reps to position their products as the best solutions for a variety of business problems. It's also standard practice for IT sales reps to seek champions within the various business units of their customer organizations. As a result of these common sales practices, IT executives such as Sweeney find themselves fielding requests for specific solutions to unspecified problems.

In some instances, however, the most appropriate solution might be a different product from the same supplier or a product from another supplier. Sometimes the customer already owns the right solution but isn't aware of it.

Occasionally, the right solution doesn't require adding new technology. Not long ago, Sweeney recalls, an executive at another bank convinced himself that he needed a document scanning system. The executive filed a request with IT, and a project manager was assigned.

The project manager asked the executive why he needed the system. The executive told the project manager that whenever his administrative assistant took a day off, he couldn't find any of his documents.

After applying the bank's IT governance processes to the request, the project manager recommended hiring a temp to file and retrieve documents when the executive's administrative assistant was absent. The project manager based his logic on a simple cost comparison. Hiring a temp would cost $25,000. Buying a document scanning system would cost $3 million.

While simplistic, the story illustrates one of the prime justifications for having IT governance processes. Without them, precious IT resources would be dissipated on projects that don't return value to the enterprise.

Perhaps a more dramatic interpretation would be something like this: Without IT governance, IT fiscal management would devolve back into the "black hole" it had been in the 1970s and 1980s. The black hole scenario would be a disaster in today's economy. So it makes sense for IT suppliers to learn as much as they can about how their customers approach IT governance and to follow the required procedures.

"Part of IT governance is making sure that things get done," Sweeney says. "Many people have asked me, 'Bill, does everything have to be a project?' Here's my reply: 'Only if you want to get it done.' There has to be a process. If there's no process, we never get where we're trying to go."

Dropping in a New Widget

All too often, IT vendors pitch products without fully considering their impact on the customer's IT infrastructure. Integration of new software with legacy systems remains a huge issue at most large companies.

"In our world, for example, every product needs to be wrapped so we can guarantee that it won't corrupt the network," Sweeney explains. "We bring the product to an engineering lab. We make sure that it installs correctly and won't take down every PC when it powers up."

Sometimes platform issues can prevent a perfectly good product from working properly. Sweeney recalls a situation in which a vendor's product ran on only one type of operating system. "We support that platform, but it's not our standard. Our internal processes were not built around it, so there were database and security issues. We plugged in the vendor's product, we powered it up, and nobody could use it."

In today's technology space, there are few stand-alone products. In a modern IT environment, everything is connected to everything else. Yet many vendors seem incapable—or unwilling—to think beyond the box they're selling. Says Sweeney:

> *This is a real problem with vendors. They'll come up with a new widget. It does exactly what it's supposed to do—when it's all by itself. They'll drop their new widget into our infrastructure, where it has to connect with 15 or 16 other systems. Then it suddenly becomes my problem, and I'm scrambling to get this widget to work with our finance systems, our market risk systems, our credit systems, our compliance systems, and our legal systems.*

Sweeney believes that most vendors still perceive their roles too narrowly. "They'll say to me, 'Bill, you asked us to come in and install a commodities trading system. And we did.' But they didn't anticipate all these infrastructure problems and they didn't help me solve them. And now I've got someone mad at me because everything is supposed to go live in 30 minutes."

Are We on the Same Page?

Like many IT executives, Sweeney has worked on both sides of the fence. A former IT consultant, he understands the pressures and challenges confronting IT sales reps. But he doesn't pull his punches when describing the inherent tension between buyers and sellers.

"The goal of the sales rep is selling software. My goal is making sure that his products work in our environment and that they deliver value or create a competitive advantage for us."

Too many times, though, "the vendor caves to a date," says Sweeney. If the customer tells the sales rep that the product he's buying must be up and running by the end of the third quarter, the sales rep will feel extreme pressure to say yes—even when it's not practical.

Trying to meet an impractical or impossible timetable can undo a relationship, especially if the implementation is rushed and problems occur.

"Never confuse sales with delivery," quips Sweeney. But there's truth beneath his jest. When a customer proposes a date that just won't work, the sales rep needs to summon up his or her courage and explain that it cannot be done. From the IT governance perspective, honesty is more than a virtue. It's an absolute requirement.

Don't Assume the CIO Is a Governance Expert

The plain truth is that not every CIO you encounter will be an expert in IT governance. Their range and depth of knowledge on the subject will vary widely, depending on their individual experience, their personality, their education, and their organization. As Thornton May puts it, "I'm not certain that all CIOs have a good feel for how IT governance works in practice."

This represents an opportunity. Smart IT suppliers should develop high-level content about IT governance and include it in their sales presentations.

Since you know that IT governance is a crucial area and you cannot assume that every CIO brings the same level of knowledge, experience, and interest to the table, you should take responsibility for raising the subject and leading the conversation.

Like it or not, IT suppliers need to step up and provide thought leadership in this area. The easiest and most practical way to generate thought leadership content—which can be presented in the form of white papers, executive summaries, case studies, or panel discussions—is by mining your own history of customer experiences.

Your history and that of your sales organization are vast reservoirs of stories, anecdotes, lessons, and cautionary tales that can be converted into thought leadership content. Don't be shy about leveraging the wisdom you've already acquired in your relationships with other customers. Take it as an article of faith that your audience is intently interested in hearing what you have to say.

Don't be afraid to develop a "political map" of critical relationships within the CIO's organization. The CIO might not know who is responsible for making key decisions and might not fully understand the scope of the interrelationships required.

Be prepared to guide the CIO through the complexities of the IT governance process. Take it upon yourself to help the CIO "stay out of hot water" by avoiding missteps and identifying potentially sticky issues before they escalate into problems that can hurt the CIO's career.

We said it earlier and we'll say it again: Be a mentor to the CIO. Help the CIO negotiate the perils and pitfalls of the corporate landscape. We guarantee that you will earn the CIO's gratitude and build a lifelong relationship.

Chapter SEVEN

When the CIO Wears the Sales Hat

"The main challenge is always trying to demonstrate to people that they've got an important role to play and that you're not just trying to shove something down their throats."

Paul J. Cosgrave

Commissioner, New York City
Department of Information
Technology and
Telecommunications (DoITT)

Role Reversals

As the duties of the modern CIO expand to include business transformation and change management, CIOs increasingly find often themselves promoting or selling IT services. Tech-savvy companies such as Boeing, Northrop, and Lufthansa have created new revenue streams by taking IT services developed internally or by subsidiaries and marketing them to external customers.

Whether the CIO's customers are internal or external, an IT vendor must be ready to provide expert knowledge and hands-on assistance to support the CIO's efforts. Moreover, today's CIO is expected to possess the political acumen of a C-level corporate officer. Modern CIOs must build support and seek buy-in from broad constituencies, manage complex relationships at multiple levels across the enterprise, and continually sell IT initiatives to ensure their success.

Jeffrey Neville, the CIO at Eastern Mountain Sports (EMS) in Peterborough, New Hampshire, says the process of generating buy-in for a project should begin in the planning stage. "Prior to starting a project we get agreement from all of the stakeholders in the business," says Neville.

EMS is one of the nation's leading outdoor specialty retailers, with more than 75 retail stores and a growing online presence. The company is committed to an aggressive strategy of continual business transformation. In addition to maintaining a rapidly expanding infrastructure, Neville and his team serve as full-time change agents.

Fortunately, the company's IT governance process ensures that new projects are prioritized in a rational way. "All the VPs sit on the governance board. When we look at a project, we take into account all of the standard measures, such as ROI. But we also score cross-functional initiatives higher. That means they're more likely to get funding, buy-in, and commitment." Granting higher priority to cross-functional initiatives encourages collaboration across departments and accelerates the pace of business transformation.

As IT penetrates more deeply into the company's daily operations, Neville's role becomes even more demanding. Before implementing an enterprise-wide project, he seeks advice and support from the director of human resources. Why HR? Because IT and HR are the only two departments that routinely touch all parts of the enterprise on a daily basis. HR is more likely to see how cross-functional IT projects will affect other parts of the organization and how various departments within the organization will respond to changes in the IT architecture. That kind of insight can be absolutely crucial to a CIO.

Like IT and HR, vendors also interact routinely with many different parts of an organization. Those interactions generate insights that can be extremely useful to the CIO.

Whether you work for the CIO, work with the CIO, or sell products and services to the CIO, consider yourself responsible for supporting the CIO's efforts to sell initiatives into a diverse and sometimes fractious market of stakeholders.

Be prepared to help the CIO anticipate and cope with common roadblocks. Supporting the CIO when these roadblocks appear—and they surely will—will demonstrate your understanding of the CIO's environment and enhance your standing as a trusted advisor.

It's your responsibility to help the CIO spot potential problems before they become insurmountable and to suggest practical tactics for overcoming obstacles. Don't wait for the CIO to tell you about a problem or roadblock. By then it's probably too late. As the old saying goes, "Expect the unexpected." See Figure 7.1.

The Selling Never Stops

Despite their evolving responsibilities, many CIOs still regard sales and marketing processes with a certain amount of

Pushback on Potential Projects and Change Initiatives	
Common Problems	**Examples of What the CIO Is Likely to Hear**
Lack of financing	Let's hold off on this purchase until our numbers improve.
Lack of support from executives and users	Top management and key users aren't interested, so I just can't sell this idea.
Fear of change	It's not broken, why fix it? We're doing okay.
Emotional issues	Linux? Are you nuts?
Divisional conflicts	What works for them won't work for us. We are just too different.
Philosophical differences	Why should we buy this, when we could just as easily build it (or vice versa)?
Ghost of projects past	We've had some bad experiences with this kind of technology in the past.
Occupational uncertainty	How will this help me in my career?
Global issues	Have you considered how this will affect our operations in Sri Lanka? Or Guatemala?
Regulations and processes	How will this affect our compliance with Sarbanes-Oxley? Or the Patriot Act? Or Gramm-Leach-Bliley?
Disagreements over perceived value	I don't understand exactly what value this project will bring to this organization.
Lack of time and attention	I've got five minutes to spare. Explain this project to me quickly while we walk to my next meeting.
Resource constraints	Great idea, but we don't have the bandwidth right now.

Figure 7.1 Every project generates some degree of pushback. Be prepared to help the CIO deal with it calmly, constructively, and effectively.

disdain. Don't allow their lack of sympathy to dissuade you from offering them a helping hand. Whether they admit it or not, they need your help.

Even when you're dealing with a CIO who feels comfortable wearing the sales hat, the chances are good that you possess experience and expertise that's worth sharing. Your willingness to share your knowledge will earn you the CIO's trust and gratitude.

"We're constantly selling our services internally," says Fred Wedley, CIO of the Long Island Rail Road. "It is an ongoing process."

A seemingly endless cycle of new regulations and mandated upgrades keeps Wedley and his team busy. Every improvement generates a cascade of integration challenges. New applications must work smoothly within the agency's existing infrastructure and must be accepted by the LIRR's community of users.

"We had problems in the past when the IT department took the lead on technology issues and we lost sight of our customer base," says Wedley. "Today we keep the focus on our customers."

Wedley comes from an IT and operations background, and he understands the LIRR's need for round-the-clock IT service. "We recently went through the process of implementing a corporate asset management strategy," he recalls. "IT had selected a package that fit the needs of the organization, but had not sold the approach to individual departments."

As a result, people who weren't involved in the selection process felt excluded. Suddenly, a decision that had seemed straightforward and logical was creating internal strife. In addition, there was genuine concern that the organization would not successfully complete corporate implementation.

To improve the approach, the LIRR set up an IT governance process. Under the process, three standing committees meet regularly to review and analyze IT needs. See Figure 7.2.

Standing IT Committees of the LIRR	
Technology Committee	**Role**
IT staffers and user representatives	Surfacing and discussing IT-related issues
Business User Council	
Business users and major operating departments	Reviewing and discussing IT needs at the departmental level
Executive Council	
EVPs, senior management	Setting organization-wide IT policy and making final decisions on major IT purchases

Figure 7.2 Sometimes committees can be a great way to make sure that crucial information is shared across the organization. Find out when the committees meet and ask the CIO if you can attend.

The committee structure allows for continual dialogues among the railroad's various departments. The committee structure also creates clear pathways for communicating and establishes a formal, transparent process for sharing information and reaching decisions affecting the entire organization.

The Executive Committee has overall responsibility for making corporate decisions. "Once the Executive Committee makes a decision, all parties accept the decision because they know it's been thoroughly and openly discussed," says Wedley. "You don't have one department establishing a non-integrated approach."

The standing committees also create forums for ongoing dialogues between the IT department and its users. Those dialogues help Wedley's team eliminate potentially unpleasant surprises that can result in ruffled feathers and loss of efficiency.

In a very direct sense, the committees make it possible for Wedley to sell the concept of standardized IT processes throughout a complex organization composed of many departments and operating units.

The LIRR is a transportation agency within the Metropolitan Transportation Authority (MTA). Wedley meets monthly with his CIO counterparts at other agencies of the MTA to stay focused on big picture issues such as overall application usage, customer satisfaction, and security. "In a large organization like ours, you build trust by maintaining open communication," he says. "That requires constant dialogue with a highly diverse audience."

When organizations adopt formal processes and structures for enabling communication among their component units, they open doors of opportunity for savvy IT suppliers. Make good use of these openings by understanding the roles of the various committees and by proactively helping the CIO's team sell programs and initiatives to its audience of stakeholders and customers.

Don't wait for the CIO to ask for your help. Make the offer. You'll find that it's worth the extra effort.

The Commissioner of Synergy

Paul J. Cosgrave serves as commissioner of the New York City Department of Information Technology and Telecommunications (DoITT). A native New Yorker, Cosgrave has devoted a career to using the power of technology to make organizations more effective.

After more than 30 years of experience in both the public and private sectors, including three years as CIO of the Internal Revenue Service, Commissioner Cosgrave is now responsible for managing the world's largest and most complex municipal IT service operation.

DoITT provides service and support for the vast archipelago of agencies that compose city government. As the department's commissioner, one of Cosgrave's primary jobs is selling the idea of centralized, integrated IT services across the city's vast bureaucracy. Says Cosgrove:

> *City government is a very complex structure. There are some 80 different agencies, offices, boards and authorities, each with its own mission and its own traditions. My chartered role at DoITT is bringing some synergy to the process. Basically, we're trying to make city services transparent, accountable and accessible to all New Yorkers.*

DoITT operates the 311 system, which essentially functions as a colossal 24/7 help desk for anyone with non-emergency questions about municipal services in the five boroughs of New York City.

"311 is our landmark," Cosgrave says with obvious pride. "311 takes all the city's customer-facing responsibilities and pulls them together under one roof. It's truly a best practice."

Before 311, people with questions or complaints about garbage, noise, or broken street lights would have to search through the telephone directory in the hope of finding the right agency to answer their questions.

In the old days, for example, if you saw an open fire hydrant, you probably would call the New York City Fire Department. While that would have seemed a logical course of action, it wouldn't have solved the problem. Eventually, you would discover that you were supposed to call the Department of Environmental Protection to get the hydrant fixed.

Meanwhile, hundreds of gallons of water could have spilled onto the street.

"311 took a bunch of 9-to-5 operations that weren't really set up to handle customer calls and consolidated them into a fully professional 24/7 call center," says Cosgrave. "It is a transformational project."

A transformational project has a deep, wide-ranging, and permanent impact. Shepherding such projects through their various stages requires the skills of a masterful executive. In many respects, Cosgrave represents the future of IT management. At DoITT, technology is a mere component in a much larger framework of people and processes held together by a common vision.

Share the Vision, Not Just the Goal

Getting the 311 system up and running in a city the size of New York City was no simple task. One of the early hurdles was convincing numerous local community boards that it was in their best interests to participate—even when it required them to yield a degree of local power.

In the absence of a central operation for processing complaints, the city's 59 community boards had become important channels for transmitting complaints to City Hall, which gave the boards influence in their neighborhoods.

"They may have initially been wary of the idea of a centralized system," Cosgrave recalls, "but I've met with them, opened the process and explained how they will become power users of the 311 system, as we develop ideas to move it to the Internet. That has helped turn the tide, and now the boards are working with us to implement the new system."

Cosgrave uses the story to illustrate a crucial point: Even in the most complicated IT scenarios, technology is rarely the primary issue. "In fact, technology is almost never the main challenge," he says. "The main challenge is always trying to demonstrate to people that they've got an important role to play and that you're not just trying to shove something down their throats."

In addition to managing the 311 system, DoITT also manages the city's web site (NYC.gov), its broadcast television station and five municipal cable channels, and a huge fiber network. DoITT is also overseeing the launch of the New York City Wireless Network (NYCWiN), which will give the city's emergency responders high-speed data access to support large file transfers, fingerprints, mug shots, city maps, and full-motion, streaming video.

"All of that gives me a certain amount of leverage that a traditional CIO might not normally have," says Cosgrave. While the additional leverage makes its easier for Cosgrave to encourage cooperation among various departments and agencies, it's not a magic wand. One of his ongoing challenges is convincing a few remaining city agencies to accept a centralized e-mail system.

"The ability to retrieve something as simple as an e-mail message is critical to any government. At the same time, you have to remember that people become uncomfortable when they feel like they're losing control. So you need to find a way to sell them on the idea."

Cosgrave says that he tries to win over hesitant agency managers by arguing that a centralized service architecture is more economical, secure, and flexible than a loosely knit collection of point applications. My message to the agencies is this: You focus on the mission-critical tasks and I'll concentrate on the infrastructure," he says. "Sometimes it's an easy sell, and sometimes it isn't. In some agencies, people dig in their heels and don't want to change. It can be challenging, but you can succeed by convincing them that they're not losing control."

Sometimes the issues can be extremely granular. "We've had debates over who owns which piece of equipment, right down to the components of a LAN (local area network)," Cosgrave says.

Service level objectives can reduce tensions and overcome internal obstacles, he adds. "People are more comfortable when you put it in writing. Service levels give you specific goals to measure yourself against. You can track your performance and prove that you're honoring your commitments."

DoITT is also charged with improving the city's 911 system. Here again, the major challenge is making sure that the stakeholders buy into the execution plan and understand how their roles and responsibilities fit into the overall vision.

The 911 project puts all of Cosgrave's skills as a technologist, strategist, and salesperson to the test. "As in any sales situation, the buyer's perception of value is crucial to the deal," he says. "So I keep selling the benefits."

Don't Be Afraid to Be Political

Back in high school, nobody wanted to be called a "politician." "Being political" or "playing politics" were definitely considered uncool.

We're not in high school anymore. Politics isn't a dirty word. It is the art of getting someone to see another person's point of view, make logical compromises, and cooperate. Politics is what makes it possible for diverse groups of people to work together and achieve shared goals.

All successful executives are political. They have to be, or they don't last. Consider the differences between Jeffrey Immelt, the CEO of GE (General Electric), and Robert Nardelli, the former CEO of Home Depot.

Both men had been groomed by Jack Welch for the top job at GE. But when it came time for Welch to hang up his spurs, he tapped Immelt as his successor.

Why did he pick Immelt over Nardelli? In retrospect, the answer seems clear. Smooth, articulate, and worldly, Immelt had the political abilities necessary to steer the world's pre-eminent megaenterprise. Welch deemed that Nardelli, de-spite his legendary street smarts and tough demeanor, just wasn't skillful enough to pilot GE.

As most of you know, Nardelli left GE and became the CEO of Home Depot. Alan Murray, a columnist for the *Wall Street Journal*, wrote a superb piece on the limitations of Nardelli's old school approach in today's business environ-ment. The modern executive, writes Murray, "has to play the role of a politician, answering to varied constituents."

Nardelli's inability to function as a political animal con-tributed more to his demise at Home Depot than the contro-versy over his hefty compensation package, according to Murray's analysis.

> *. . . subsequent events have confirmed the wisdom of Mr. Welch's choice. Like Mr. Nardelli, Mr. Immelt has struggled with a languishing stock price. But in addition to generating good operating results, Mr. Immelt has played the CEO's po-litical role with great skill. He has tied his own pay closely to performance. He has eschewed the kind of employment con-tract that is now rewarding Mr. Nardelli. He has reached out to a wide range of constituent groups.*

As a result, writes Murray, "Mr. Immelt wins awards, graces magazine covers, and is widely praised as one of America's best CEOs."

There's a lesson here for all of us who work in the IT universe. We pride ourselves on being smart, savvy connoisseurs of high technology. But to a far greater extent than any of us would rather imagine, our success increasingly depends on our abilities to get along with people who don't always agree with us and who don't immediately see the value in what we're doing.

It would be difficult to find a CIO today who isn't involved in some kind of enterprise-wide effort to standardize operating platforms or centralize critical business functions. Those types of projects are inherently political because they involve the redistribution of power and influence.

Our interviews with Fred Wedley and Paul Cosgrave clearly demonstrate the advantages of using good old-fashioned political tactics to persuade diverse groups of constituencies to embrace a common vision.

As the role of the CIO becomes less about managing technology and more about enabling business transformation, CIOs without finely honed political skills will find themselves severely disadvantaged. Since politics is a form of selling, IT vendors are perfectly positioned to provide genuinely useful advice and counsel to their CIO customers. Don't be shy about sharing your experiences, and don't be afraid to offer the CIO tips for winning over difficult customers. There will be many instances in which the true nature of the challenges facing a CIO will be more apparent to you, the vendor, than to the CIO. There's no reason why you can't serve as a political mentor to the CIO.

Selling Up, Down, and Sideways

Bruce C. Barnes, the president and CEO of Bold Vision, learned the hard way that selling a new IT concept requires 360 degrees of effort, especially at a large organization.

Previously in his career, Barnes was the CIO at a global enterprise where a crucial IT project had languished for years under several earlier leadership teams. "Now it was my turn in the barrel," recalls Barnes. Mindful of the project's significance and aware that its high visibility would make it vulnerable to sniping, Barnes received permission to report directly to the CEO for the duration of the project.

With the CEO's approval and support, Barnes swiftly made a series of changes in staffing, suppliers, schedules, and organization. "Clearly I had achieved legitimate power and was positioned for success," he remembers thinking. "I figured intuitively that if the CEO was on board, I was golden."

Then the roof fell in. While Barnes focused on implementing the project, an angry director caught the ear of the CEO and convinced him that Barnes' plan was too disruptive. The director talked the CEO into purchasing a solution from a vendor whom Barnes had cast aside earlier. Barnes says:

I should have found a way to get the director more involved in the project. People have a way of getting even with you, especially if you try to run over them. What I failed to appreciate was that I needed the cooperation of many people in the organization who had been members of the prior leadership team. Without their buy-in, I couldn't succeed.

Barnes realized belatedly that the challenge he faced was more political than technological. Even though the CEO had granted him permission to make sweeping changes, making those changes stick required more political skill than he could muster at the time.

"What I should have done was figure out how to make people understand what they had to gain and how they would benefit. I needed to make their pain go away without creating more work for them. Instead, I did just the opposite. It was a real eye-opener and I've never forgotten it."

The fact that the solution Barnes had rejected turned out to be a clunker doesn't change the basic lesson: The CIO needs political skills to sell the message of change and transformation. "Vendors can assist by putting themselves behind the eyeballs of the CIO. The CIO is surrounded by people with different needs, different goals and different agendas. Help the CIO become the ringleader who pulls it all together and you will be the hero."

It's not easy for CIOs to become political animals overnight. Some CIOs are further down the path than others. Vendors can help by providing early warnings to the CIO when political challenges appear on the horizon. Vendors should be prepared to offer useful suggestions for resolving internal political issues and should offer coaching to improve the CIO's political skills.

Vendors should remind CIOs that IT is no longer seen as a magic black box that can be mysteriously dropped onto someone's desk. IT has joined the mainstream and people expect IT executives to obey all the natural laws of social behavior.

Here are the questions that a wise CIO will pose to the people around him as he considers moving ahead with a complex IT project:

- What will make you a hero in your organization?

- What do you see as the home run here?

- What are your goals for this project?

- What's your vision for resolving the challenges we face?

- What do you want to accomplish five years down the road?

Shaping Demand

Are CIOs worried that if they do a better job of selling and marketing IT services, they will be creating more work for themselves? That's what Thornton May believes. "Many CIOs already hold the sales process in low esteem. And when they read books about marketing, the books all talk about 'creating demand.' To the average CIO, 'creating demand' translates into 'creating more work.' Naturally, they don't see that as a good thing."

Indeed, creating demand is not an issue for most IT departments. They've already got plenty. "On the other hand, the CIO needs to manage and influence demand for IT services," says May. "The CIO needs to have his or her hand firmly on the demand throttle."

To avoid becoming passive riders on a runaway train of accelerating demand, CIOs need more control of the demand creation process. "CIOs need to begin shaping demand for IT services," says May. "Right now, people are demanding the wrong things from IT. And as we've seen, demand for IT can be infinite. CIOs must learn how to exert more influence over demand or risk being overwhelmed."

Convincing large constituencies of users to adopt new methods of sharing essential information technologies won't be easy. "People will have to give up their fiefdoms and let go of their old mental models," says May. "It won't be easy."

Organizations will look to their CIOs to guide them through the arduous process of transformation. But will their CIOs rise to the challenge?

In an era of continual transformation, agents of change require ultrasharp political and leadership skills. "You're really talking about the CIO becoming a cultural diplomat, a true politician with the ability to build consensus and agreement out of potential chaos," says May.

The purely rational strategies favored by many technology executives won't work since there will be too many conflicting versions of reality to resolve. "The job will be changing how people think about IT. Vendors can help by mapping the needs of the stakeholders and creating the template for a new mental model of how we view IT," says May.

May likens the process to a combination of cultural anthropology and nation building. "The end goal is changing human nature," he says.

Chapter EIGHT

Inside the Mind of a CIO

"Show me how the $1 million we spend with you is going to generate $10 million in value for our company and you'll get my attention very quickly. Talk to me about chipsets or bandwidth and I'll start yawning."

Paul Zazzera
Former CIO, Time Inc.

Letting Go of the Past

Every industry has its own set of special traditions and shared memories. The IT industry is no different. We long for the good old days, and occasionally we wish that the pace of change would slow down just a bit.

A sense of nostalgia is probably healthy, and it's okay to enjoy our memories of easier times when the divide between vendors and their customers seemed narrower. But as Mark Hall notes in his excellent foreword to this book, many IT suppliers seem to be stuck in the past, at least as far as their sales processes are concerned.

That is not a good thing. Like it or not, the times they are a-changin'. IT suppliers with outmoded or antiquated sales processes will find themselves increasingly at a disadvantage as their target audience opts for competitors with greater empathy and deeper business acumen.

The CIOs and other experts whom we quote in this book represent a tiny sample of the worldwide market for IT products and services. But they speak volumes about the issues and challenges facing IT suppliers today, and their words offer sound advice that's worth considering seriously.

We sincerely hope that *Partnering with the CIO* will inspire a fresh dialogue about the state of IT sales and will accelerate the process of change required for the good of all parties involved.

Change is invariably painful, because it always involves loss. But transformation is the name of the game, especially in the technology sector. The CIOs we interviewed look forward to working with IT suppliers who understand their issues and who are willing to partner with them in a search for effective solutions.

Many IT suppliers have already launched the processes required to transform themselves from sellers into partners. We applaud their efforts and we wish them good fortune. If your company is still relying on outdated techniques to sell IT products or services, we urge you to discreetly place a copy of this book on the desk of your vice president of sales.

Since *Partnering with the CIO* begins with a brief story told to us by Paul Zazzera, we think it is appropriate to conclude the book with a chapter based on one of our conversations with him. We found his observations illuminating, and we trust that you will, too.

Buying by the Pound

Experienced CIOs like to say they can remember when companies bought computer equipment by the pound. "The computers were what we bought and the software was thrown in, almost like an afterthought," says Zazzera. "Back then, we all talked about automation and efficiency."

Paul Zazzera began his tech career in 1980, when heavy iron—bulky computers and the equipment required to keep them running—dominated the IT landscape. Tracy Kidder captures the essence of that era perfectly in *The Soul of a New Machine.*

> *But computers were relatively scarce, and they were large and very expensive. Typically, one big machine served an entire organization. Often it lay behind a plate glass window, people in white gowns attending it, and those who wished to use it did so through intermediaries. Users were like supplicants. The process could be annoying.*

Anyone who lived through that era remembers the painful gap between the promise of computing and the reality of computing. Fortunately, the IT landscape began changing radically in the early 1980s. Driven largely by the higher expectations of younger managers and enabled by an extraordinary series of advances in semiconductor technology, IT evolved beyond the mainframe and entered a new, exciting era.

By the time Zazzera joined the party, some far-sighted companies had already replaced their mainframes with client–server systems. Some really bold companies had gone even further, replacing their legacy architecture with networked PCs.

Despite exhilarating progress, most people still viewed IT as a truly black art, shrouded in mystery and managed by nerdy guys who enjoyed watching reruns of *Star Trek*. Top management generally regarded IT as a necessary but decidedly secondary function.

At most corporations, IT was relegated to the periphery. It was seen as another cost center, like building maintenance or transportation. In those days, no one spoke of IT as a core competency, and only a handful of visionary companies saw IT as an engine for strategic growth.

IT vendors exploited all those prejudices, transforming them into huge, long-lasting advantages for their sales teams. By the mid-1980s, most companies knew that IT was becoming increasingly important, but few could say with any precision how much IT or what kind of IT they really needed. So they bought and bought, knowing they would never be held accountable for their spending decisions.

It was a great market for IT vendors. The woods were full of semi-knowledgeable prospects with fat wallets. The balance of power between the vendors and their customers seemed permanently tilted in favor of the vendors. It would take more than 20 years for the balance to shift.

Tail Fins and Flashing Lights

"When I started in this business, they sold IT the way Detroit sold cars. The big difference was that computers were never equipped with chrome-plated bumpers and tail fins," says Zazzera. "But like cars, computers were often sold on the basis of size and speed. The bigger, faster ones had to be better, right? It also helped if there were flashing lights. The standard sales pitch rarely included a discussion about whether all that additional size and speed would actually lead to measurable gains in productivity. Very few people really cared."

By the middle of the 1980s, however, opinions and beliefs about the intrinsic value of information were changing. Spurred by a growing consensus that information should be treated as a valuable asset, companies began stocking up on IT. Suddenly the vendors couldn't keep up with demand as companies raced to buy all kinds of IT products and services—whether they actually needed them or not.

The arrival of the desktop PC brought millions of new users into the IT universe, which accelerated the IT shopping spree that had begun a few years earlier. The unexpected popularity of the Internet, the World Wide Web, and e-mail sent IT budgets soaring to new and amazing heights. Everyone on the planet, it seemed, had become an IT consumer.

By the mid-1990s, the world was wired. Sober people spoke seriously about "the new economy," in which global markets, ubiquitous computing, and 24/7 access to information would eliminate traditional business cycles. There would be no more recessions. The stock market would keep rising. Poverty would be erased. War would become obsolete.

Replacing the "Big Sponge" Model

"Twenty-five years ago, there was nothing out there," recalls Zazzera. "You had a marketplace that was, quite honestly, like a big sponge. The digital revolution was just beginning, and everyone was struggling to get their hands on new technology."

Obviously, the market has changed since then. "Now everyone has technology. Everyone has networks. The basics are in place. We can be global, we can be mobile. We can work from anyplace we want. We're no longer impressed by the technology. We just want to know how the technology is going to help our business."

Zazzera echoes the sentiments of almost every CIO we spoke with. Not interested in buying features or functionality, they're interested in buying results.

"Show me how the $1 million we spend with you is going to generate $10 million in value for our company and you'll get my attention very quickly," he says. "Talk to me about chipsets or bandwidth and I'll start yawning."

That doesn't mean that Zazzera is totally bored by technology. It simply means that any sales pitch that doesn't address a specific business issue isn't likely to work. Talk to him about solving a real business challenge and he'll listen.

If you're a vendor, I want you to talk to me about how you're going to help us do a better job of up-selling and cross-selling our customers. I want to hear about how you're going to help us deliver our services in new and exciting ways. I want to hear about some new way for reaching customers that we've never imagined and that no one else is doing. I want you to tell me that you can help us extend our brand and break into new markets.

RECOMMENDED READING

Broadbent, Marianne, and Ellen S. Kitzis. *The New CIO Leader: Setting the Agenda and Delivering Results.* Boston: Harvard Business School Press, 2005.

Fugere, Brian, Chelsea Hardaway, and Jon Warshawsky. *Why Business People Speak Like Idiots: A Bullfighter's Guide.* New York: Free Press, 2005.

Keen, Jack M., and Bonnie Digrius. *Making Technology Investments Profitable: ROI Road Map to Better Business Cases.* Hoboken, New Jersey: John Wiley & Sons, 2003.

Kidder, Tracy. *The Soul of a New Machine.* New York: Little, Brown and Company, 1981.

Kim, W. Chan, and Renee Mauborgne. *Blue Ocean Strategy: How to Create Uncontested Market Space and Make the Competition Irrelevant.* Boston: Harvard Business School Press, 2005.

Kotter, John P. *John P. Kotter on What Leaders Really Do.* Boston: Harvard Business School Press, 1999.

Lutchen, Mark D. *Managing IT as a Business: A Survival Guide for CEOs.* Hoboken, New Jersey: John Wiley & Sons, 2004.

Sheth, Jagdish, and Andrew Sobel. *Clients for Life: How Great Professionals Develop Breakthrough Relationships.* New York: Simon & Schuster, 2000.

Smith, Gregory S. *Straight to the Top: Becoming a World-Class CIO.* Hoboken, New Jersey: John Wiley & Sons, 2006.

ABOUT THE AUTHORS

Michael Minelli is a successful sales professional and client advisor. He manages clients for SAS Institute, the world's largest privately owned software company and the global market leader in business intelligence. He lives in Westchester County, New York, with his wife Jenny and their two children.

Mike Barlow is an award-winning journalist, media relations professional, and co-author of best-selling business books. Since launching his own firm, Cumulus Partners, he has represented major organizations in numerous industries. He lives in Fairfield County, Connecticut, with his wife Darlene and their two children.

INDEX